Fourth Edition

Counseling Strategies and Interventions

Harold Hackney
Fairfield University

Sherry Cormier
West Virginia University

Allyn and Bacon
Boston • London • Toronto • Sydney • Tokyo • Singapore

*This book is lovingly dedicated
to our children:
Kirsten, Jason, and Curtis
Christiane and Lisanne*

Series Editor: Ray Short
Series Editorial Assistant: Christine M. Shaw
Editorial-Production Administrator: Annette Joseph
Editorial-Production Coordinator: Susan Freese
Editorial-Production Service: TKM Productions
Manufacturing Buyer: Megan Cochran
Cover Administrator: Linda K. Dickinson
Cover Designer: Suzanne Harbison

Copyright © 1994, 1988, 1979, 1973 by Allyn and Bacon
A Division of Simon & Schuster, Inc.
160 Gould Street
Needham Heights, Massachusetts 02194

Library of Congress Cataloging-in-Publication Data

Hackney, Harold
    Counseling strategies and interventions/Harold Hackney, Sherry
Cormier. —4th ed.
        p.   cm.
    Includes bibliographical references and index.
    ISBN 0–205–14800–X
    1. Counseling.   I. Cormier, L. Sherilyn (Louise Sherilyn)
    II. Title.
BF637. C6H25   1993
158' .3—dc20   92–33891
                                                          CIP

Printed in the United States of America

10 9 8 7 6 5 4 3 2   98 97 96 95 94

Contents

Exercises

Preface

Since the third edition of *Counseling Strategies and Interventions*, the counseling profession has continued to expand and evolve. An increasing number of training programs have been recognized by various accrediting bodies. For example, professional counseling programs are now accredited by the Council for Accreditation of Counseling and Related Educational Programs (CACREP); counseling and clinical psychology programs are accredited by the American Psychological Association (APA); marriage and family counseling programs are accredited by the American Association of Marriage and Family Therapists (AAMFT); and social work programs are accredited by the Council on Social Work Education (CSWE). All of these organizations monitor the type, duration, and quality of training that helpers receive throughout their training and educational processes.

In writing this fourth edition, we have kept several features from the previous editions. First, we have tried to be comprehensive yet concise. Second, the book has been written with upper-class undergraduates or beginning-level graduate students in mind. Also, we have included a variety of learning exercises to help students apply and review what they have learned.

At the same time, we have made some changes, including deletions and additions. We have eliminated out-of-date material and added content that reflects new sources and new thinking about the field. Many recently published sources are included. There is also an increased emphasis on the impact of gender and cultural issues in counseling.

A great number of introductory-level texts are now published in the counseling field—many more than existed when we published our first edition. What we believe makes this book unique is the emphasis on and integration of the person of the counselor and the counselor's skills, strategies, and objectives. We believe that the two are interrelated. An effective counselor is one who has both the necessary personal qualities as well as certain skills and strategies to offer in dealing with various clients and their issues. We have continued to emphasize this sort of interrelation in the fourth edition.

Chapter 1 identifies the context of professional counseling—who the professional counselor is and what kinds of activities he or she enters. This context includes a wide variety of roles and functions. It might even seem to the untrained eye that the differences among helpers are greater than the similarities. We attempt to dispel that impression in Chapter 2, where we discuss the helping relationship. It is this helping relationship that proves to be the unifying force for disparate roles and functions.

Although the helping relationship connotes a sense of shared purpose, there is an added expectation for the counselor—the expectation that he or she be both responsible and responsive in exploring the client's needs and concerns. In Chapters 3 through 10, we identify the skills and interventions expected of a beginning professional counselor. Some of these skills are rudimentary; others are more advanced and require coaching and practice. Chapters 3 and 4 define the counselor's responsibility to be aware of and responsive to the client's communication patterns. Effective attending skills place the counselor in a responsible role in the counseling relationship. This responsibility is examined in Chapter 5, which deals with session management.

Chapters 6 through 8 delineate the basic counseling strategies designed to elicit, support, or direct client change. Whether the focus be the client's thoughts, attitudes, or feelings, or more likely a combination of all three, the counselor has certain tools or skills that facilitate the client's growth. Often these skills enable the counselor to understand the client's problem or the client's world.

Chapter 9 is a pivotal point in the book. It builds on the fundamentals of the early chapters and is the foundation for the remaining chapters of the book. Although the counselor is instrumental in conceptualizing problems (usually with the assistance of a particular theoretical orientation), the goal-setting process is inherently dependent on *mutual* discussion and agreement between counselor and client. Drawing on mutually accepted counseling goals, the counselor begins the most crucial portion of the relationship—the focus on overt change. This calls for more than relationship skills and more than active listening. There are many counseling interventions—derived both from theory and practice and supported by research—that are synonymous with effective counseling. In Chapters 9 and 10, we explain and suggest classroom activities that will help the reader to understand and begin practicing these interventions.

Finally, Chapter 11 focuses on the process of clinical supervision and how beginning counselors may use it to advance their skills. Counselor educators have long used clinical supervision skills in the training of counselors, but the specificity of those skills and the inclusion of the trainee as a participant in successful clinical supervision has not been dealt with in most professional texts. This chapter was authored by Janine Bernard.

As you begin the process of understanding the role of helper and as you acquire the necessary skills required for effective helping, you will come to realize that the ultimate goal is to develop your abilities to the point that they are a natural extension of your existing interpersonal skills. But this will not be the case in the beginning. The interventions and even the conceptualizations may seem unnatural, inconsistent with your existing behaviors, or inappropriate. As you become more accomplished in the craft of counseling, these counseling skills will begin to feel more comfortable, appropriate, and effective. Ultimately, they will become a natural part of your professional practice.

H. H.
S. C.

▶ 1

The Helping Profession

The helping profession includes a broadly knit collection of professionals and paraprofessionals, each fitting a particular need or segment of society. Some are directly identified as helping professionals, such as psychiatrists, psychologists, professional counselors, marriage and family therapists, and social workers. Others are professionals from other disciplines who enter the helping network for temporary periods of time. Most notable among these are ministers, physicians, nurses, and teachers. When discussing the helping profession, it is important to keep this fluid interplay between career helpers and peripheral helpers in mind. The bond they share is a desire, a need, or even a mission to be of help. This helping activity has both a subjective and an objective quality and can be studied from both perspectives.

Most counseling textbooks devote at least a portion of one chapter to the subject of helping. You might think that a process so inherent to human nature as this act of extending oneself to another person should be self-evident. And yet people continue to belabor the subject in ways not unlike the poet who talks about love. In a psychotherapeutic context, the process has carried many labels, among which are *treatment, analysis, facilitation,* and *modification.* In the company of such terms, the label *helping* seems innocently harmless, if not simplistic. In fact, the act of helping proves not to be so simple or clear to the participant or observer.

WHAT IS HELPING?

The process of helping has several dimensions, each of which contributes to the definition of *helping*. One dimension specifies the conditions under which helping occurs. Another dimension specifies the preconditions that lead one person to seek help and another to provide help. Yet a third dimension relates to the results of the interaction between these two persons.

Helping Conditions

The conditions under which helping occurs are quite complex, but in their simplest terms may be described as involving "(a) someone seeking help, (b) someone willing to give help who is (c) capable of, or trained to help (d) in a setting that permits help to be given and received" (Cormier & Hackney, 1992, p. 2).

The first of these conditions is obvious; one cannot help without the presence of someone seeking help. If I don't want to be helped, nothing you can do will be helpful. If I'm not sure I want to be helped, then perhaps you will be helpful, provided you can enjoin me to make a commitment to accept help.

Many clients experience pain, rage, and frustration because from an early age their needs have been thwarted or blocked (Teyber, 1992). This is particularly true for persons who grew up in families where there was a great deal of conflict, stress, and/or impaired boundaries (i.e., explicit or implicit rules that serve to separate parts of a family system). In an effort to adapt and survive within this family unit, such persons usually adopt one or more roles that are in some way more protective of the family than of oneself as an individual (Miller, 1981). The individual's own needs are often lost in an effort by the entire family to keep the family system in balance. Such persons as clients are highly adept at noting and responding to the needs of others, including their counselors. At one level they may consciously even wish to focus some of their attention on the counselor's needs because this feels familiar to them. For example, some clients may be very solicitous about a therapist's well-being. However, at another level, these clients might be enraged if the counseling process simply repeats what has happened to them in their own families, and that is that their needs become secondary or overlooked. In the helping process, it is critical for the counselor to be aware of and to monitor his or her own needs as the helper.

The second condition requires the willingness or intention to be helpful. Here it would be good to differentiate between the *intention* to be helpful and the *need* to be helpful. Many would-be helpers are driven by the need to be helpful and use the helping relationship for their own ends. This is rarely a conscious act. Neediness has a way of camouflaging itself in more respectable attire. But when the relationship is dictated by the helper's needs, the possibilities for helping are minimal.

It is important to recognize and accept your needs. All people have needs for such things as intimacy, power, esteem, admiration, and so on. It is also important to be certain that you are not dependent on your interactions with clients for fulfilling these needs in a primary way. One of the best ways to ensure that you do not depend on clients inappropriately to meet your needs is to take care of yourself and to live a balanced life in which your needs are met through relationships with a partner, family, friends, or even a support group of other helpers. If you are living your own life in a healthy and balanced way, then your clients will not have to provide you with intimacy, approval, and admiration and will be free to receive from you the kinds of things that *they* need.

The third condition reflects the counselor's skills, either learned or natural. It is not enough to be well intentioned if your awareness and behaviors drive people away. The fourth condition, a setting in which help may occur, refers to the physical surroundings in which the helper and client meet. Conditions such as privacy, comfort, aesthetic character of the room, and timing of the encounter all contribute to the setting in which helping transpires.

Carl Rogers (1957) has discussed the "necessary and sufficient conditions" for helping to occur. His description included conditions similar to those listed above. But he also added some personal qualities of the counselor (accurate empathy, unconditional positive regard) and a communication issue—that the client be able to perceive the counselor's understanding and respect for the client. We discuss these relationship conditions in greater detail in Chapter 2.

SETTINGS IN WHICH COUNSELORS WORK

If one takes into account the nonprofessional helper, then helping can occur wherever two or more people might meet. But with our focus on paraprofessional and professional helpers, the locations tend to be institutionalized; that is, they tend to be in settings that reflect continuing and ongoing service delivery. Furthermore, they tend to be located close to specific target populations for which they are intended. The following discussion of representative settings and the services they perform will provide some sense of the helping spectrum.

Counseling in School Settings

School counselors are found in elementary, middle or junior high schools, and high schools. Elementary school counselors do provide some individual counseling with children, but they are more likely to work with the total school environment. Much of the elementary school counselor's focus is on working with the teaching staff to construct a healthy psychological environment in the school for young children. This is accomplished through teacher conferences, classroom presentations, parent conferences, and talking to the children (Ohlsen, 1983).

Middle school and junior high school counselors share this total school perspective but tend to spend more time with students, individually and in groups, and somewhat less time with teachers and parents. This slight shift in focus reflects the developmental changes that occur with preteens, who find themselves involved in self-exploration and identity crises.

Counseling in the high school reflects a noticeable shift to the student as an individual. Career and college planning, interpersonal concerns, family matters, and personal identity issues tend to dominate the student's awareness, and the counseling process attempts to provide an environment in which these issues may be addressed. The counselor's day is therefore much more task oriented. Some students are referred by teachers, but many students are self-referrals. The high school counselor often works with student groups on career and college issues, but individual contact is the main medium for other concerns.

Counseling in College Settings

Most college counseling occurs in counseling centers or psychological services centers. A wide variety of problems are addressed, including career counseling, personal adjustment counseling, crisis counseling, and substance abuse counseling. College counselors also see students with mild to severe pathological problems ranging from depression to suicide gestures to eating disorders. In addition to individual counseling, much reliance is placed on group counseling and on training paraprofessionals to run crisis telephone services and peer counseling programs. In writing about this population, Utz has noted that many of the problems of adult life have their beginnings at the college age. As a result, "the college counselor has an opportunity to help students when problems would seem more manageable and subject to change" (1983, p. 169).

Counseling in Community Settings

Counselors working in community settings usually are master's degree–level social workers (M.S.W.) or mental health counselors (M.A.). Their places of employment are the most diverse of all counseling settings. They "may be in private practice or they may be employed in one of a variety of community agencies, ranging from the large community mental health center with a staff of specialists trained to deal with many types of situations, to the small one- or two-person office which has limitations to the types of clients it serves" (Ohlsen, 1983, p. 297).

Family service agencies, youth service bureaus, satellite mental health centers, YWCA counseling services, and substance abuse centers are examples of what one finds in community settings. Much of what is done is psychotherapy, whether with individuals, families, or groups. In addition, the community counselor may become involved in community advocacy efforts and direct community intervention. The types of problems seen by community counselors encompass the spectrum of mental health issues. Clients include children, adolescents, adults, couples, families, and the elderly. In other words, community counselors see an enormous variety of clients and problems in a typical month. The work demands are often heavy, with case loads ranging from 20 to 40 clients per week.

Counseling in Religious Settings

Counseling in religious settings is in many ways similar and in some ways different from that in other counseling settings. The religious counseling center often is associated with a particular denomination (for example, Catholic Family Services, Methodist Family Counseling Center, Jewish Family Services). The similarities include the range of individual and family problems seen, the types and quality of therapy provided, and the counselors' professional qualifications. The differences reflect the reasons why some religious groups establish their own counseling services. There is at least some acknowledgment of the role of religion or God in the individual's life problems. Many religious counselors believe that human problems must be examined and changes introduced within a context of religious beliefs and values. The religious counseling center is undeniably attractive for many clients who, because of their backgrounds, place greater trust in the counselor who works within a religious affiliation.

Counselors in religious settings often are ordained ministers who have obtained postgraduate training in counseling. But increasing numbers of the laity are also entering religious counseling settings. Their training may be similar to that of the community mental health counselor or the marriage and family therapist.

Counseling in Industrial Settings

Many professionals consider the private sector to be the new frontier for counseling services. Forrest (1983) described this movement as a response to industry's need to deal with employee personal problems that negatively affect job performance. Counseling services occur primarily in the form of Employee Assistance Programs (EAPs) that are administered either within the plant or through a private contract with a counseling agency. EAPs are occurring with increasing frequency in business, industries, governmental units, hospitals, and schools (Forrest, 1983). Although the primary focus of most EAPs is the treatment of substance abuse problems, some have expanded into other types of personal and family problems.

In addition to employee assistance programs, a new type of counseling service has appeared in industry settings: the outplacement counseling service. *Outplacement* refers to the process of facilitating the transition from employment to unemployment or from employment in one corporation to employment in another. The need for outplacement counseling is increasing as corporations streamline their operations to cut costs or to address new goals and objectives. The client may be a top executive, middle manager, line supervisor, or laborer. Counseling takes the form of career counseling and includes the administration of career and personality inventories. The objectives for management clients are (1) to provide data and counseling that will help executives assess their career options and develop plans for obtaining new positions and (2) to support clients through that transition period. The objective for plant employees who may be affected by plant closings is to identify career alternatives for the employees and to assist the company in designing retraining programs that will help the unemployed workers obtain new jobs. Much that is done in outplacement counseling is similar to what a career counselor would do. But the outplacement counselor is usually a person who has worked in an industry setting and understands the characteristics of this clientele from firsthand experience.

Counseling in Health Care Settings

An increasing number of counselors are finding employment in health care settings such as hospitals, departments of behavioral medicine, rehabilitation clinics, and so on. Responsibilities of helpers in these settings include such diverse things as providing counseling to patients and/or patients' families, grief work with the terminally ill, and the implementation of psychological and educational interventions for patients with chronic illnesses, persons with physical disabilities, and so on.

INGREDIENTS OF PROFESSIONAL COUNSELING

We have described six settings in which professional counseling occurs. There are many others, of course, including marriage and family therapy, rehabilitation counseling, correctional institution counseling, employment counseling, and geriatric counseling. In all of these settings, and with the variety of presenting problems that are seen, there is a common core of counselor characteristics, skills, and abilities. These common ingredients may be categorized as the personal qualities of the counselor, the counselor's interpersonal skills, the counselor's discrimination/conceptual skills, and the counselor's intervention skills.

The Counselor's Personal Qualities

What are the raw materials, the predisposing conditions that contribute to the development of a highly skilled counselor? Do all counselor trainees possess these raw materials? Corey, Corey, and Callanan have observed that "a counselor's values, beliefs, personal attributes, life experiences, and way of living are intrinsically related to the way he or she functions as a professional" (1988, p. 28). They identified 10 personal qualities that are found in effective counselors:

1. Good will—a sincere interest in the welfare of others
2. The ability to be present for others; the ability and willingness to be with them in their experiences of joy and pain
3. A recognition and acceptance of one's personal power; being in contact with one's own strength and vitality; without need to diminish others or feel superior to them
4. The knowledge that one has found his or her own counseling style, that style being an expression of one's own personality
5. A willingness to be vulnerable and to take risks
6. Self-respect and self-appreciation; a strong sense of self-worth
7. A willingness to serve as models for their clients
8. A willingness to risk making mistakes and to admit having made them
9. A growth orientation
10. A sense of humor (pp. 28–30)

In addition to these qualities, two others are worth considering. One is the counselor's ability to promote the welfare of the client. Another related and personal quality involves open-mindedness and flexibility—that is, the capacity to hear, believe, and respond in an open and nonjudgmental fashion to clients who may have values, beliefs, and lifestyles different from your own. This quality is especially important in being able to work effectively with clients of the opposite gender or of a different ethnic origin and with clients with alternative lifestyles including sexual orientation.

As we discussed earlier in this chapter, part of being an effective counselor also involves the awareness of your own needs and the ability to put the well-being of your clients first. Helpers in all fields are guided by codes of ethical behavior (*Ethical Standards*, American Counseling Association, 1981; *Ethical Principles of Psychologists*, American Psychological Association, 1992; *Code of Ethics*, National Association of Social Workers, 1979; and *Code of Ethical Principles for Marriage and Family Therapists*, American Association for Marriage and Family Therapy, 1985). A major guiding principle of all of these ethical codes is the recognition of the importance of being committed to the client's well-being.

The Counselor's Interpersonal Skills

Although personal qualities are basic ingredients for good counseling, possession of these qualities alone does not ensure that one will be a successful counselor. There is a second level of characteristics that determine how a counselor is able to relate to others. Egan (1990, pp. 61–74) described some of these qualities as pragmatism, competence, respect, genuineness, and the promotion of client self-responsibility. Other interpersonal skills include the ability to listen and to communicate accurately what one has heard without becoming dominant in the interaction and being able to communicate one's competence, trustworthiness, and sensitivity to the other person's situation. This array of characteristics must contribute to a general ability to put clients at ease, to elicit client trust, and to work through difficult moments, tasks, and problems.

The Counselor's Discrimination/ Conceptualization Skills

As the counseling relationship evolves, the counselor becomes increasingly involved in the client's personal world. From the client's perspective, the counselor *becomes* part of his or her world. This involvement challenges the counselor to be in the relationship and yet to remain objective. Such a challenge is very difficult because it requires the counselor to exhibit congruence, honesty, and professional responsibility, all at the same time.

The counselor must be able to listen, to comprehend, to relate, to think through, to recognize connections and contradictions, to conceptualize what these might mean within some theoretical framework, to react, to instigate, to support, to challenge, and to empathize—all within the span of a counseling session. And this must all be done as believably as it is felt. Otherwise, the counselor will take on a phony or incongruent persona.

The Counselor's Intervention Skills

Finally, counselors must be able to implement their conceptualization of what would facilitate the client's growth and success with presenting problems. It is our belief that "all counselors, regardless of theoretical orientation, have a therapeutic plan that they follow, a plan that is related to the assessment of the presenting problem, to their view of human nature and change processes, and to the resulting goals that have been agreed upon" (Cormier & Hackney, 1992, p. 29). These interventions may address the client's feelings and attitudes, the client's thought processes and assessments of life situations, the client's behaviors or efforts to change, or the client's interpersonal relationships and the effect those relationships have.

Some intervention skills are nothing more than common sense and are as common among friends as they are in counseling. Other interventions are unique to the therapeutic relationship and are formed out of the theoretical conceptualizations of human relationships. As counselors grow in experience and training, their repertoire of intervention skills grows and their ability to recognize when and how to introduce interventions increases.

TRAINING OF COUNSELORS

We have already indicated that professional counselors are trained in graduate programs, usually affiliated with higher education institutions, that lead to a master's degree. Traditionally these programs have required 33 semester credits, but recently most of them have been upgraded to require 48 to 60 semester credits. These latter programs may be designed to meet professional criteria established by the Council for Accreditation of Counseling and Related Educational Programs (CACREP).

Most training programs begin with a series of courses that introduce the helping professions, settings, client populations, and professional ethics. Early in most programs a counseling techniques laboratory or prepracticum introduces students to communication skills and entry-level counseling interventions, and provides opportunities to try out these skills in an observable setting (either through a two-way mirror or a closed-circuit video). Such a course includes content that is presented in this text. Typically, this course is followed by a counseling practicum in which students work with real clients under the supervision of a skilled counselor or therapist. That supervision may include live observation, videotaped review, or audiotaped review. Whatever the medium, sessions are reviewed by the supervisor, and feedback is provided to the trainee to permit assessment and professional growth.

Concurrent with these courses, most students take courses in group counseling (sometimes including a group practicum), psychology, educational and psychological testing, and career counseling and development.

Toward the end of the program, many trainees are required to complete a one-year internship in a counseling setting related to their program. This may be in school counseling, agency counseling, college counseling, or another related setting. Programs in social work and marriage and family therapy differ in some of the didactic content, but the experiential portions are similar.

SUMMARY

We have examined the meaning of helping in the context of human problems and who the helpers are. Professional helpers are found in many settings and encounter a wide variety of human problems. The effective helper brings to the setting certain personal qualities, without which the client would not likely enter into the alliance in which help occurs. But more than personal qualities are necessary for one to be a professional helper. One must possess certain interpersonal skills, conceptual skills, and intervention skills to be an effective counselor. While the exact parameters of these skills may be defined by the counselor's theoretical orientation, there is no denying that the effective counselor has them and the ineffective counselor does not.

In the chapters that follow, we shall examine these skills and provide you with exercises and discussion questions to help in your integration of the material. Chapter 2 will look at the helping relationship and conditions that enable it to develop in positive directions to facilitate the client's progress. Chapters 3, 4, and 5 address the interpersonal skills of the counselor in regard to attending to clients, recognizing communication patterns, and managing the counseling session. Chapters 6, 7, and 8 focus on the cognitive and affective messages of clients and ways in which counselors can differentiate between and respond to these two types of messages. Chapters 9 and 10 address the counselor's skills in conceptualizing problems and selecting and implementing strategies and interventions. Finally, Chapter 11 looks at the special issues involved in supervisor-trainee sessions, with the aim of helping the beginning counselor to make full use of the benefits of supervision.

DISCUSSION QUESTIONS

1. In a small group of three to five class members, each of you should identify a preferred setting in which you would choose to be a professional counselor. Discuss among yourselves why you chose the particular setting. Does it have to do with your personal qualities? Your

perception of the demands of the setting? Your perception of the rewards of working in that setting?

2. Now choose a second-most-preferred setting (other than your first choice). Continue the discussion as directed in Question 1. How did you find your reactions to be different in this second discussion? What might you learn from these differences? Did you perceive the other group members as having similar or different reactions to the second choice? What did you learn about them as a result? Share your reactions candidly.

3. Identify a person you have known who was, in your opinion, an exceptional helper. What qualities did this person possess that contributed to his or her helping nature? How do you think these qualities were acquired? Do you have any of these qualities?

4. In your opinion, what does it mean to help? To give help? To receive help? How are these processes related?

5. What has impacted your decision to become a helper? Consider the following sources of influence: your family of origin (the one in which you grew up), life experiences, role models, personal qualities, needs, motivations, and pragmatic concerns.

RECOMMENDED READINGS

Baruth, L. G. (1985). *Counseling and psychotherapy.* Columbus, OH: Merrill.

> *This basic text in counseling covers a variety of topics related to counseling and the helping process.*

Corey, M. S., & Corey, G. (1989). *Becoming a helper.* Pacific Grove, CA: Brooks/Cole.

> *This book explores the stresses and roles of helpers in working with clients.*

Fong, M. L. (1990). Mental health counseling: The essence of professional counseling. *Counselor Education and Supervision, 30,* 106–113.

> *Fong offers a clarification of the work of mental health counselors as the foundation of professional counseling.*

Gerstein, L. H., & Brooks, D. K., Jr. (1990). The helping professions' challenge: Credentialing and interdisciplinary collaboration. *Journal of Counseling and Development, 68,* 475–523.

> *This special feature issue describes recent trends and issues in the credentialing of counselors, psychologists, social workers, and marriage and family therapists.*

Goldenberg, I., & Goldenberg, H. (1991). *Family therapy: An overview* (3rd ed.). Pacific Grove, CA: Brooks/Cole.

This classic text in family therapy gives an overview of the role, interventions, and settings used by family therapists.

Hohenshil, T. H., & Szymanski, E. (1989). Counseling persons with disabilities: 10-year update. *Journal of Counseling and Development, 68,* 138–179.

This special feature issue describes a number of settings of rehabilitation counselors and the work they do.

Lewis, J., & Lewis, M. (1992). *Community counseling.* Pacific Grove, CA: Brooks/Cole.

This book describes community counseling settings and the functions of community counselors.

May, G. (1987). *Simply sane: The spirituality of mental health.* New York: Crossroad Publishing.

May describes an enlightening view of what occurs in the helping process.

Sauter, S. L., Murphy, L. R., & Hurrell, J. J., Jr. (1990). Prevention of work-related psychological disorders. *American Psychologist, 45,* 1146–1158.

This article describes a number of ways in which mental health needs arise and can be addressed through counseling and psychological intervention in the workplace.

Teyber, E. (1992). *Interpersonal process in psychotherapy* (2nd ed.). Pacific Grove, CA: Brooks/Cole.

Part III of this book, "Conceptualizing Client Dynamics," discusses in great detail the characteristics and needs of clients and presenting dynamics.

Woodside, M., & McClean, T. (1992). *An introduction to human services.* Pacific Grove, CA: Brooks/Cole.

This book describes the role and function of the human services worker and is particularly helpful for those in social work settings.

▶ 2

The Helping Relationship

Much of what is accomplished in counseling is dependent on the quality of the relationship between the counselor and the client. In all the writing on this subject, none offers more than an approach to helping known as the *person-centered approach.* This approach has been described by Corey:

> *The person-centered approach focuses on clients' responsibility and capacity to discover ways to more fully encounter reality. Clients who know themselves best are the ones to discover more appropriate behavior for themselves based on a growing self-awareness. The approach emphasizes the phenomenal world of the client. With an attempt to apprehend the client's internal frame of reference, therapists concern themselves mainly with the client's perception of self and of the world. (1991, pp. 208–209)*

The person-centered approach derives principally from the work of one individual: Carl Rogers. Rogers emerged on the counseling scene at a time when two psychological approaches, psychoanalysis and behaviorism, were dominant. Through his influence, the profession began to focus on the relationship between therapist and client, as opposed to the existing emphasis on either the client's intrapsychic experience or patterns of behavior. In one of his early writings, Rogers (1957) defined what he believed to be the "necessary and sufficient conditions" for positive personality change to occur. These conditions referred to characteristics inherent in a constructive interpersonal relationship, including accurate empathy, unconditional positive regard, and genuineness. These concepts have evolved over the years, and today they are generally acknowledged by most theoretical approaches as core conditions in the therapeutic process.

In addition to these core conditions, the helping relationship has an intentional dimension. Hansen, Stevic, and Warner described this intentional nature as

> *an alliance formed to help the client move toward a goal: more appropriate behavior. The client is able to try changes through an internalization of this therapeutic alliance. The internalization is made possible by the counselor's acceptance of the client as a person and by the former's help in resolving a problem.* (1986, p. 234)

In this chapter we shall examine the helping relationship, taking into account both the core conditions and the notion of intentionality.

ACCURATE EMPATHY

There are numerous definitions of *empathy* in the counseling literature. The one that we like is the following: the ability to (1) understand the client's experience and (2) feel with or emotionally resonate to the client's experience as if it were your own but without losing the "as if" quality (Rogers, 1957; Barrett-Lennard, 1981; Greenberg & Goldman, 1988).

Empathic understanding involves two primary steps:

1. Accurately sensing the client's world; being able to see things the way he or she does
2. Verbally sharing your understanding with the client

How do you know when the client feels you have understood? Client responses such as "Yes, that's it" or "That's exactly right" indicate some sort of recognition by the client of the level of your understanding. When your clients say something like that after one of your responses, you are assured that they feel you are following and understanding what is occurring.

Learning to understand is not an easy process. It involves the capacity to switch from your own set of experiences to those of your clients, as seen through their eyes, not yours. It involves sensing the feelings they have, not the feelings you have or might have had in the same or similar circumstances. It involves skillful listening, so that you can hear not only the obvious but also the subtle shadings of which, perhaps, even the client is not yet aware.

Empathy also involves having good internal boundaries for yourself. An internal boundary helps to separate personal thoughts, feelings, and behaviors from the thoughts, feelings, and behaviors of others (Mellody, 1989, p. 11). Rogers (1957) asserted that empathy is being sensitive to a client's experiencing a feeling. You can feel with the client yet you do not take on the client's feelings and actually feel them yourself. This is an area that occasionally poses problems especially for beginning counselors.

In your eagerness to be helpful, you may find yourself becoming so involved with the client that you get disconnected from yourself and what you are feeling. Instead, you take on the client's feelings and perhaps even find yourself obsessing about the client long after the session is over. Such *immersion* is not helpful because you lose your capacity to be objective in a subjective way about the client's experience. As a result, you may avoid seeing, hearing, or saying important things in the session. If you feel this is happening to you, you can talk it over with a supervisor. You also can get reconnected to yourself during a session by taking a minute to focus internally and privately on what you are feeling and by taking some deep breaths.

Understanding clients' perspectives alone is not sufficient. You also must express verbally to clients your sense of understanding about them. This kind of communication is, in effect, a kind of mirror—feeding back clients' feelings to them, without agreeing or disagreeing, reassuring or denying. Accurate empathy involves not only mirroring the client's feelings but also some parts of the immediate process. For example, if clients continually ask many questions, rather than discuss the issues that brought them to counseling, it would be appropriate to reflect on the obvious with statements such as:

"You have a lot of questions to ask right now."

"You seem to be wanting a lot of information about this."

"You are asking a lot of questions. I wonder if you are uncertain about what to expect."

Learning to develop accurate empathy with your client and with other people takes time and practice. You must experience the client's feeling first, understand it as best you can, then react to it by using your own words.

Cultural Empathy

In addition to understanding the client's verbal message, it is also important to consider the impact of gender and cultural backgrounds. There is increasing evidence that men and women talk in different ways (Tannen,

1990) and that cultural/historical backgrounds affect the meaning the client conveys as well as the meaning the therapist interprets. For example, suppose the client is a Puerto Rican woman who is in an unhappy marriage and the counselor is a Caucasian Anglo-American Protestant male who has been twice divorced. Because of their gender, cultural, and historical differences, without acute sensitivity to these differences on the counselor's part, "the two may be talking to each other but the degree of understanding may, at times, be so slight that in truth two cultures [and genders] are talking 'by' each other and the individuals are lost in the process" (Ivey, Ivey, & Simek-Downing, 1987, p. 97). To facilitate an increased empathic response to clients of different genders and cultures, it is important for counselors "to generate a maximum number of thoughts, words, and behaviors to communicate with a variety of diverse groups" (p. 97). This expansion in your own communication allows you to understand the experience of people who are in very different life situations from your own.

▲ EXERCISE 2.1: ACCURATE EMPATHY

See what you can do to *hear* the client accurately and to communicate your perceptions to the client.

A. Hearing and Verbalizing Client Concerns

Using triads with one person as speaker, a second as respondent, and the third as observer, complete the following tasks. Then rotate roles until each person has had an opportunity to react in all three ways.

1. The speaker should begin by sharing a personal concern or issue with the listener.
2. The respondent should
    a. listen to the speaker and account for gender, cultural, and historical factors as well as the verbal message.
    b. verbalize to the speaker what he or she heard.
3. The observer should note the extent to which the others accomplished their tasks and whether any understanding or misunderstanding occurred.

Following a brief (five-minute) interaction, respond verbally to the following questions:

Speaker: Do you think the respondent heard what you had to say? Did you think he or she understood you? Discuss this with the respondent.

Respondent: Did you let the speaker know you understood or attempted to understand? How did you do this? What blocks within yourself interfered with doing so?

Observer: Discuss what you saw taking place between the speaker and the respondent.

Now reverse roles and complete the same process.

B. Understanding Client Concerns

This exercise should be completed with a group of 3 to 10 people sitting in a circle.

1. Each participant is given a piece of paper and a pencil.
2. Each participant should complete, in writing and anonymously, the following sentence: My primary concern about becoming a counselor is

<u>What if I don't like the student I'm counseling?</u>

3. Papers are folded and placed in the center of the circle.
4. Each participant draws a paper. (If one person receives his or her own, all should draw again.)
5. Each participant reads aloud the concern listed, then talks several minutes about what it would be like to have this concern. Other participants can then add to this.

This process continues until each participant has read and discussed a concern. When discussing the concern, attempt to reflect only your *understanding* of the world of the person with this concern. Do *not* attempt to give a solution or advice.

After the exercise, members should give each other feedback about the level of empathic understanding that was displayed during the discussion. Sometimes it is helpful to have all group members rank each other as to who showed the most understanding, who showed the least, and so on. Feedback should be specific so participants can use it for behavior change.

Shame and the Empathy Bond

Another factor that is increasingly recognized as having a substantial impact on the helping relationship is shame. Shame is viewed as a central component or main regulator of a person's affective life. Normal shame is about values and limits; it is recognized, spoken about, and acknowledged. The shame that is considered pathogenic and a primary contributor to aggression, addictions, obsessions, narcissism, and depression is hidden shame—shame that is unacknowledged, repressed, or defended against that seems to result in either an attack on others or an incredible self-loathing (Karen, 1992).

According to Lewis (1971), shame is inescapable in the counselor-client relationship and has major implications for the empathic bonding of the counselor to the client. Karen quoted Lewis as follows: "However good your reasons for going into treatment, so long as you are an adult speaking to another adult to whom you are telling the most intimate things, there is an undercurrent of shame in every session" (1992, p. 50). Lewis (1971) asserted that not only do counselors overlook shame in clients and bypass dealing with it but they inadvertently add to a client's "shame tank" through judgmental interpretations. She stated that when this happens, the client becomes enraged at the counselor but, because he or she cannot accept feeling angry toward someone who is a "helper," it is turned inward and becomes depression and self-denigration. Lewis cautioned counselors to be alert to client states of shame so that they can help clients work through and discharge the feeling. In this way, clients can move ahead. Otherwise, they are likely to continue to move in and out of shame attacks or shame spirals, both within and outside of the counseling sessions.

A major precursor to shame appears to be the lack of parental empathy. According to Miller (1985), a child's sense of self-esteem comes largely from the parents' capacity to tune in empathically with the child, to mirror and reflect the child as she or he develops. As Karen pointed out, in therapy, "the same phenomenon requires a special sensitivity on the part of the therapist. The patient is hypersensitive about acceptance and abandonment and uncertain of whether he can trust the therapist with his wound—a wound that, he no doubt senses, the therapy session has great potential to exacerbate. The therapist must win over the hiding, shameful side of the personality and gradually help it to heal" (1992, p. 65). The counselor does this by creating an empathic bond with the client—that is, an emotional connection, a genuine feeling for the client. Although empathy can be conveyed by certain techniques (such as the verbal expressions we noted earlier), ultimately there is no substitute for the counselor's ability to genuinely care for and feel with the client.

POSITIVE REGARD

In his early writings, Carl Rogers (1957) described positive regard as unconditional. That quality has been interpreted by Hansen, Stevic, and

Joan
Develop
3,23,1422 P1329

✓ 6
Feb.
P 86

✓ 10
Nov/Dec 91 P53

150.
150. 82 H255 g
370.152 MS99F

Warner as "respect[ing] the client regardless of differences in values, differences in how one sees the world; in short, no condition is set upon the client's behaviors and experiences" (1986, p. 112). Lietaer (1984) observed that this is "probably one of the most questioned concepts in client-centered therapy," noting that "there is a potential conflict between genuineness or congruence on the one hand and unconditionality on the other" (1984, p. 41). Perhaps for this reason, more recent writers have relabeled positive regard as "nonpossessive warmth."

Positive regard, or nonpossessive warmth, is often misconstrued as agreement or lack of disagreement with the client. Instead, it is an attitude of valuing the client. To show positive regard is to express appreciation of the client as a unique and worthwhile person. It is also to be noncritical, to provide an "overall sense of protection, support, or acceptance, no matter what is divulged" (Karasu, 1992, p. 36). As Karasu noted, unconditional or positive regard specifically means that the client's supposedly bad or unacceptable ideas, wishes, and feelings can be expressed without loss of the counselor's respect and attention. In other words, the client can divulge whatever is needed and still be protected from the counselor's "personal reactions, especially those that reflect rejection or disdain" (p. 37).

▲ EXERCISE 2.2: POSITIVE REGARD

A. Overcoming Barriers to Positive Regard

Think of expressing to the client (1) those limitations that may be blocking your sense of liking for the client and (2) those strengths that increase your appreciation for the client. The following steps may assist you in expressing this:

1. Picture the other person in your mind. Begin a dialogue in which you express what it is that is interfering with your sense of positive regard. Now, reverse the roles. Become the other person. What does the person say in response? Then what do you say?
2. Complete the above process again. This time express the strengths you see in the other person, what you appreciate about that person. Again reverse the roles. Become the other person. What does he or she say in response? Then what do you say?

This exercise can be used with any client toward whom you have difficulty experiencing positive regard.

B. Expressing Positive Regard

Take a few minutes to think of a person with whom you currently have a relationship and for whom you experience positive regard. What kinds of things do you do to express your feelings of positive regard for this person? Jot them down.

I missed you!
I'm so proud of you!
It's so nice to see you!
I enjoy talking with you!

There is no set answer to the exercise above because each person has a different style of communicating good feelings for another person. The first step, though, is positive regard—to feel comfortable enough to *express* warm feelings to someone else. Being free enough to spontaneously share feelings of regard for another human being is a process that can be learned.

Think again for a moment about several of your existing relationships with a few people close to you—perhaps your spouse, parent, child, neighbor, or friend. Then respond, in writing, to the following questions:

What is your level of expression of positive regard to these people?

How often do you say things like "I like you"; "It's nice to be with you"; "You're good for me"; "I enjoy you"; and so forth?

What is your feeling when you do?

What is the effect on the other person?

If your expression of these kinds of statements is infrequent, what might be holding you back?

Either now or later, seek out someone you like and try to express these kinds of feelings to that person. Then think again about the previous questions. Share your reactions with your partner.

In doing this you will probably note that warmth and positive regard are expressed both nonverbally and verbally. Nonverbally, they are shown by facial expression, smiling, and eye contact. In fact, you might think of your entire nonverbal stance as communicating a degree of enthusiasm for the other person.

In counseling, positive regard is sometimes shown when the physical posture of the counselor mirrors that of the client. Verbally, you express your feelings for another person by statements that reflect a sense of caring and affection, best described, perhaps, by the word *nurturance.* Affectional nurturing statements can have a strong effect on the client and on the relationship. They are most effective when used *selectively* and *sincerely*. You know the feeling you have about someone who is always saying nice things—these statements lose their effect when used constantly.

Some examples of affectional nurturing statements are:

Client:	"I know I shouldn't do that because at those times I'm selfish, yet it's hard for me to always do everything for her first, but I am selfish and that's an even worse way for me to be.
Counselor:	"I like you even when you're selfish."
Client:	(Crying) "I'm sorry I'm crying. They [parents] tell me I am a baby for doing it, but I am so worried, but uh, I'll try not to do it."
Counselor:	"It's all right for you to cry with me."

Think of some affectional nurturing statements on your own. List them below and discuss them with someone.

I want to help you,
It's ok to make mistakes,
You're a special person.
I'll always be your friend.

GENUINENESS

The notion that the counselor should project genuineness is also difficult to define. Rogers tended to connect it with *congruence,* a condition reflecting honesty, transparency, and openness to the client. Rogers and Truax described counselor congruence in the following way:

> In relation to therapy, [congruence] means that the therapist is what he is, during the encounter with the client. He is without front or facade, openly being the feelings and attitudes which at the moment are flowing in him. It involves the element of self-awareness, meaning that the feelings the therapist is experiencing are available to him, available to his awareness, and also that he is able to live these feelings, to be them in the relationship, and able to communicate them if appropriate. It means that he comes into a direct personal encounter with his client, meeting him on a person-to-person basis. It means that he is being himself, not denying himself. (1967, p. 101)

The beginning counselor may find this condition easier to apply in theory than in practice. Questions such as "What if I really don't like my client? Should I let that be known? Wouldn't it destroy the relationship?" rise inevitably when genuineness and congruence are examined. The appropriate answer to these questions may not be entirely satisfying. Genuineness dictates that the counselor be honest, but in helpful, rather than destructive, ways.

There is much more to genuineness than an occasional encounter with a disagreeable client. Many beginning counselors fall into the trap of playing the counselor's role by merely reflecting the client's feelings. Limiting your expression and involvement to this set of responses presents several problems:

1. It creates insecurity; the client is kept in a constantly ambiguous state about how you feel.
2. There is no role-model effect for the client. If you can effectively express *your* immediate feelings, it encourages the client to do likewise.
3. There is no source of feedback other than the client's perceptions. Expression of your feelings gives clients an idea of how they are perceived by others.

Expression of your feelings should not take precedence over understanding the client's feelings. The counseling relationship does not have all the mutuality that is present in many other relationships, such as friend to friend, husband to wife, and so forth. Sharing your feelings is most beneficial when it serves one of the three purposes mentioned above.

Before you can express your feelings, you must become aware of them. For example, ask yourself what it means to be genuine. Can you tell when you are being yourself or when you are presenting an image that is different from the way you actually feel? In order to communicate genuineness to the client, you must first learn to get in touch with yourself and your feelings—to become aware of who you are as an individual and what kinds of thoughts and feelings you have. This involves learning to discriminate between your various feelings and allowing them to come into your awareness without denial or distortion; it means, for example, that when you are happy you can acknowledge that you are happy and when you are angry you can be aware of your anger.

▲ EXERCISE 2.3: DYADIC ENCOUNTER

To assist you in becoming aware of your own thoughts and feelings, select a partner and spend a few minutes with this dyadic encounter experience (Banikiotes, Kubinski, & Pursell, 1981). It is designed to facilitate getting to know yourself and another person on a fairly close level. All you need to do is respond to the open-ended questions as honestly and directly as possible. Both of you should respond to one question at a time. The discussion statements can be completed at whatever level of self-disclosure you wish.

> My name is _____ .
> The reason I'm here is _____ .

One of the most important skills in getting to know another person is listening. In order to check on your ability to understand what your partner is communicating, the two of you should go through the following steps one at a time.

Decide which one of you is to speak first in this unit. The first speaker is to complete the following item in two or three sentences:

> When I think about the future. I see myself . . . .

The second speaker repeats in his or her own words what the first speaker has just said. The first speaker must be satisfied that he or she has been heard accurately.

The second speaker then completes the item in two or three sentences. The first speaker paraphrases what the second speaker just said, to the satisfaction of the second speaker.

Share what you may have learned about yourself as a listener with your partner. To check your listening accuracy, the two of you may find yourselves later saying to each other, "Do you mean that . . . ?" or "You're saying that . . . ."

> When I am new in a group, I . . . .
> When I am feeling anxious in a new situation, I usually . . . .
> (Listening check:) "You're saying that . . . ."
> The thing that turns me on most is . . . .
> Right now I'm feeling . . . . (Look your partner in the eye while you respond to this item.)
> When I am rejected, I usually . . . .
> The thing that turns me off the most is . . . .
> Toward you right now, I feel . . . .
> When I am alone, I usually . . . .

(Listening check:) "Do you mean that . . . ?"
I am rebellious when . . . .

Checkup

Have a two- or three-minute discussion about this experience so far.
Keep eye contact as much as you can and try to cover the following points:

How well are you listening?
How open and honest have you been?
How eager are you to continue this interchange?
Do you feel that you are getting to know each other?
(Then continue)
I love . . . .
I feel jealous about . . . .
Right now I'm feeling . . . .
I am afraid of . . . .
The thing I like best about you is . . . .
You are . . . .
Right now I am responding most to . . . .

SELF-DISCLOSURE

Expression of your thoughts, ideas, and feelings follows after your awareness of them. This process might also be called *self-expression* or *self-disclosure.* Self-expression and disclosure are important ways of letting the client
know that you are a person and not just a role; however, self-disclosure
should be used appropriately and not indiscriminately in the counseling
sessions.

It is important not to interpret self-disclosure to mean that you ought to
talk about yourself, since the primary focus of the interview is on the client.
Thus, genuineness does not mean that you reveal your own experiences
and values. It does mean, however, that occasionally it is appropriate and
helpful for you to reveal or disclose a particular feeling you may have about
the counseling session or about the client. The clue to appropriateness is
often determined by the question "Whose needs am I meeting when I disclose this idea or feeling—the client's or mine?" Clearly, the former is the
much more appropriate instance of the two.

There are several different kinds of self-disclosure. These include:

1. The counselor's own problems
2. Facts about the counselor's role
3. The counselor's reactions to the client (feedback)
4. The counselor's reactions to the counselor-client relationship

Usually, disclosure in the latter two areas is more productive. Many times counselors are tempted to share their problems and concerns when encountering a client with similar problems. In a few instances, this may be done as a reassurance to clients that their concerns are not catastrophic. But, in most other instances, a role reversal occurs—the counselor is gaining something by this sharing with the client. Some research indicates that the counselor who discloses at a *moderate* level may be perceived by the client more positively than the counselor who discloses at a high or low level (Nilsson, Strassberg, & Bannon, 1979). Thus, too much or too little self-disclosure may limit the client's confidence in you as an effective helper.

Often clients may ask questions concerning information about the counselor: "Are you married?" "Why did you become a counselor?" "Are you in school?" These are common types of questions clients ask in seeking facts about the counselor. In this case, it is usually best just to give a direct, brief answer and then return the interview focus to the client. However, if this is a common occurrence with the same client, there are other ways of responding. Continual client questioning of this sort often indicates that the client is anxious and is attempting to get off the "hot seat" by turning the focus onto you. There are better ways to handle this than by spending the interview disclosing facts about yourself! Alternative ways of responding include:

1. Reflect on the client's feelings of anxiety: "You seem anxious about talking about yourself now."
2. Reflect on the process: "You seem to be asking a lot of questions now."
3. Make a statement about what you see happening: "I think you feel as if you're on the 'hot seat' and asking me questions is a good way for you to get off it."

▲ EXERCISE 2.4: SELF-DISCLOSURE

Think about yourself in the following instances:

1. You have a client who describes herself as shy and retiring. During the third interview she says, "I'd like to be like you—you seem so outgoing and comfortable with people. Why don't you just tell me how you got that way?" Do you then consider it appropriate to share some of your experiences with her?

2. You have had one particular client for about seven individual sessions. After the first session, the client has been at least several minutes late for each session and waits until almost the end of the interview to bring up something important to discuss. You feel that he is infringing on your time.

This is preventing you from giving your full attention and understanding to the client. You have acknowledged to yourself that this is bothering you. Is it appropriate to go ahead and express this to him?

Take a few minutes to think about yourself as the counselor in these two examples. Now write in the space below what you would do in each example to communicate *facilitative genuineness*.

① I would refocus the session on the client.

② I would express my feelings to the client.

There are no right or wrong answers to these two examples; each counseling interaction is somewhat different. Ultimately, you, as the counselor, will have to make a decision like this for yourself in each instance. Based on the preceding written material, perhaps you did indicate that it would be more appropriate to express your irritation (the second example) than to disclose your experiences (the first). In the first instance, rather than sharing facts about yourself, there are more productive ways of helping that client reach her goals. For example, she would be more involved if you suggest role reversal. You become the client; have her be the outgoing and comfortable counselor she sees. In the second instance, the client is not fulfilling his share of the responsibility by being late, or he is indirectly communicating resistance that needs to be shared and discussed.

Some counselors are able to acknowledge their feelings and determine when these can best be expressed in the interview but are not sure how to express these kinds of thoughts and feelings to the client. Self-disclosure or expressions of genuineness are often characterized by sharing and feedback statements—statements that convey to the client your sense of what is going on and your feelings about it (Ivey & Simek-Downing, 1980). These kinds of statements are illustrated by the following examples:

"I am glad you shared that with me."
"If that happened to me, I think I'd feel pretty angry."
"I don't feel that we're getting anywhere right now."

Other examples of sharing kinds of responses are :

Client: "It's hard for me to say so but I really do get a lot out of these sessions."

Counselor: "That makes me feel good to hear you say that."
                      or:
                 "I'm glad to know you feel that way."

Note that in the counselor's sharing statements, the communication is *direct*—it focuses on the counselor's feelings and on the client. It is a better statement than a generalized comment like "I hope most clients would feel the same way." Sharing and feedback statement should avoid the trap of "counselor language." To begin a sharing and/or feedback statement with "I hear you saying," "It seems that you feel," or "I feel that you feel" gets wordy, repetitive, and even phony. Say *exactly* what you mean.

▲ EXERCISE 2.5: EXPRESSING COUNSELOR FEELINGS

Sharing and feedback communicate to the client that you have heard or seen something going on and that you have certain thoughts or feelings about it that you want to communicate. Sometimes you will want to say not only what you feel about a specific instance or experience but also how you feel about the client. This will be more effective if your feelings are expressed as immediate ones—that is, expressed in the *present* rather than in the past or future. This is the meaning of keeping the process of relationship in the here and now, using what is going on from moment to moment in each session to build the relationship. It is represented by the type of statement that communicates, "Right now I'm feeling . . ." or "Right now we are . . ."

To experience this here-and-now kind of communication, try to get in touch with yourself this instant. What are you feeling *this very moment* as you are reading and thinking about this page, this paragraph, this sentence? Write down four or five adjectives that express your present feelings. Tune into your nonverbal cues as well (body position, rate of breathing, tension spots, etc.).

tired   hot   laid back

▲ EXERCISE 2.6: USING SHARING STATEMENTS

With a partner, engage in some sharing-type statements that are direct, specific, and immediate. Can you tune into your feelings as you engage in this kind of communication? What does it do for you and what effect does it have on the other person? Jot down some of these reactions here. List the sharing statements you have made to your partner.

_____

_____

_____

_____

_____

Sharing statements reflect the expression of the counselor's thoughts and feelings. Feedback statements incorporate a description of *client behavior* as well. Some examples of counselors' feedback-type statements are "When you are continually late to the sessions (client behavior) I feel it is a loss to both of us" (counselor feeling), or "When you talk about school, your face really lights up" (client behavior) and "It feels good to me to see you so happy about that" (counselor reaction).

You probably are aware as you read that these examples have several characteristics fundamental to effective feedback processes. Such statements express a feeling acknowledged and *owned* by the counselor, as in "When something happens, I feel thus and so" or "When I see you _____ I think _____." They avoid judgment and evaluation. Most of all, they do not accuse or blame, as in the following statement: "You are a real problem to work with because you are always late." In other words, they preserve the dignity and self-respect of the other person involved in the relationship. Furthermore, an effective feedback statement does not contain advice; it is not a "parenting" or scolding statement. It also should concern a behavior or attitude the other person has the capacity to change or modify. It would not be helpful, for instance, to use the following kind of feedback statement: "I just don't like the way you look. Why don't you do something about your complexion?"

Feedback is usually more effective when it is solicited. Thus, feedback statements that relate to clients' goals or to aspects of the counseling relationship may be better received by clients because of their involvement in this. In any case, though, you can determine the effects of your feedback by the clients' reactions. If your clients are defensive, give detailed explanation or justification, or make strong denials, this is a clue that your feedback was not solicited and that perhaps you have touched on an issue too soon. At this point in the relationship, clients need an indication of your support and acceptance.

▲ EXERCISE 2.7:   USING FEEDBACK STATEMENTS

With a partner, try some feedback-type statements that meet the characteristics described in the preceding section. Be sure your responses include a description of your partner's behavior as well as your reactions to it. For example, you might say something like "I appreciate (your feeling) your taking the time to talk with me (partner's behavior)."

List the feedback statements you make to your partner. What are the effects on you? On the other person? On the relationship?

_____

_____

_____

_____

A CLIMATE OF SAFETY

The primary reason why the conditions of a therapeutic relationship are so important is to help clients feel safe. When clients feel safe, they feel trusting and free to be open and disclosive. As Karasu observed, "This special permission to experience one's psychic life under the interpersonal sheath of a psychologically safe environment gives psychotherapy its unique quality, allowing the [client] to gradually shed the accumulated layers of defensive armor" (1992, p. 37). When clients do not feel safe, they often feel self-protective, guarded, and subdued. It is the counselor's responsibility to offer the kind of climate in which clients feel the sense of safety they need in order to ask for and accept help. If a client has come from a particular kind of family or relationship in which there was a lot of stress, perhaps even abuse or incest, then the counselor's efforts to provide a safe environment will need to be even more intentional and more intensive.

Clients, particularly those who have had their trust broken in the past, will often test the counselor. They will likely not believe that the therapist's initial efforts to be understanding, sincere, accepting, and warm are really true. They may want to find out if they really mean something to the counselor—if they really are valued as the therapist says they are. This reason may account for all kinds of client feelings and behaviors that are projected or reflected in or outside a session, including acting out, calling the counselor on the phone, being late to a session, becoming angry, and so on. It is as if clients long for a warm, caring empathic helper but, due to their history, fear this and in their fear, resist, attack, or retreat (Karasu, 1992, p. 21). Efforts to provide a safe therapeutic environment for clients need to be ongoing and persistent.

SUMMARY

Although the counseling relationship has some marked differences from other interpersonal relationships, it does serve as a model that the client can use to improve the quality of relationships outside the counseling room. You must assume responsibility at the outset of counseling for those qualities that generate and maintain the relationship process. Later, as the client's comfort and social skills get stronger, the relationship becomes a mutually responsible condition.

Clearly, the counseling relationship cannot succeed without the presence of accurate empathy or understanding of the client's world. When you assume that you understand, but you do not, you and your client detour from a constructive and helpful course and risk the dangers of false conclusions and failure. In a similar manner, if you do not value your client or if you do not consider the client's problems and concerns to be real, you are denying the most reliable information about your client's perceptions. Lacking this information, you cannot help your client develop in more constructive directions. Finally, and underlying both accurate empathy and positive regard, the degree to which you can be honestly and consistently yourself, knowing yourself, and sharing yourself with your client will establish the ultimate parameters of the helping relationship.

Although the behaviors presented in this chapter can be learned and incorporated into your style and repertoire, there is a dimension yet to be acknowledged. The integral human element of the counseling relationship cannot exist by mechanical manipulation of certain behaviors at given moments. Your relationship with each client contains its own uniqueness and spontaneity that cannot, without the loss of both genuineness and sincerity, be systematically controlled prior to its occurrence. Your spontaneity, however, will increase rather than decrease once you have become comfortable with a variety of counseling techniques. While you are learning counselor responses, this ease may not be quite as apparent because you will need to overlearn them. However, once the responses suggested in this book have become second nature to you, your spontaneity as a counselor will begin to emerge. You will be on your way to becoming the helper you hope to be.

DISCUSSION QUESTIONS

1. How do you approach a new relationship? What conditions do you require to be met before you open yourself to a closer relationship?

2. What were the "unwritten rules" in your family about interactions with nonfamily members? How might these rules affect the kind of relationship you are able to offer clients?

3. If you were a client, what conditions would you look for in your counselor?

4. Under what conditions do you feel safe? Open and disclosive? Trusting? Does this vary with persons of different ages, gender, values, and ethnic origin?

RECOMMENDED READINGS

Gelso, C. J., & Fretz, B. R. (1992). *Counseling psychology.* Fort Worth: Harcourt Brace Jovanovich.
Chapter 5, "The Therapeutic Relationship," offers a current overview of the primary components of the counseling relationship.

Kahn, M. (1991). *Between therapist and client: The new relationship.* New York: Freeman.
This book is one of the best all-around sources for studying aspects of the counseling relationship, with a particular emphasis on empathy.

Karasu, T. B. (1992). *Wisdom in the practice of psychotherapy.* New York: Basic Books.
This book describes a number of ways in which the therapeutic relationship impacts clients. It is organized by brief and concise points of clinical wisdom and followed up with extensive case illustrations.

Karen, R. (1992). Shame. *Atlantic Monthly, 269,* 40–70.
Karen cites a number of ways in which the concept of shame impacts the helping relationships. This is truly a cutting-edge article—a not-to-be missed reading for helping professionals.

Patterson, C. H. (1984). Empathy, warmth, and genuineness in psychotherapy: A review of reviews. *Psychotherapy, 21,* 431–438.
This article contains a summary of the various reviews of these three core relationship conditions.

Patterson, C. H. (1985). *The therapeutic relationship: Foundations of an eclectic psychotherapy.* Pacific Grove, CA: Brooks/Cole.
This book is an excellent, concise source for describing various aspects of the helping relationship.

Rogers, C. R. (1986). Rogers, Kohut, and Erikson. *Person-centered Review, 2,* 125–140.
Rogers discusses and contrasts the role of empathy in the helping relationship.

Welwood, J. (Ed.). (1983). *Awakening the heart: East/west approaches to psychotherapy and the healing relationship.* Boston: New Science Library.
This book comprises a series of articles on the helping relationship that represent a composite of Eastern thought and Western psychological practice.

▶ 3

Attending to Clients

Thus far we have identified several conditions that affect the development of the counseling relationship. Those conditions—accurate empathy, positive regard, and genuineness or congruence—are called *core conditions* because they are central to the therapeutic process. While these core conditions are necessary, the counselor must also bring other skills and knowledge to the therapeutic process. Certainly the first of these skills is the ability to *listen* actively and attentively to the client. This objective is not so simple as it might appear. It involves more than the attentive ear.

Have you ever talked to someone who was fiddling with a pencil, staring around the room, or seemed otherwise distracted as he or she listened to you? If you have—and who hasn't—you will recall how this felt. The listener may have heard all that you said, but you probably interpreted his or her behavior as a lack of interest, concentration, or attention. And, if that seemed to be the case, you may have found it difficult to continue the conversation. Clients exhibit this same sensitivity to whether the counselor is paying attention to what they say. Counseling research strongly suggests that nonverbal behavior does influence the verbal message with which it is paired, particularly when inconsistencies exist between verbal and nonverbal messages (Tyson & Wall, 1983).

This chapter is concerned with the behaviors that do or do not facilitate communication and the core conditions in counseling. In addition, attending skills used by the counselor to assure the client and to support or reinforce the client are examined. These skills are very important for the client who is feeling vulnerable, uncertain, nonconfident, or nontrusting.

One precondition for the existence of these reinforcing or supporting behaviors is an awareness of the client's communication. This awareness must then be communicated through your undistracted attentiveness to the client. Attentiveness is one way of saying, "I am following both your message and your metacommunication; I am experiencing as you are experiencing this moment; I am invested and involved in your story." Studies have indicated that attentiveness is related to other counselor attitudes, most notably empathy and involvement. Counselor interest and commitment appear to be related to clients' and observers' perceptions of the counselor's empathy and positive regard (Fretz, Corn, Tuemmler, & Bellet, 1979; Hill, Siegelman, Gronsky, Sturniolo, & Fretz, 1981).

COMMUNICATION OF ATTENTIVENESS

Attentiveness is communicated primarily through four channels: facial expressions, eye contact, body positions and movement, and verbal responses (Ivey, Ivey, & Simek-Downing, 1987). Although attending to clients on the surface appears relatively simple, it is easier said than done. Egan (1990) listed a number of obstacles to the attending process:

1. Being preoccupied
2. Being judgmental
3. Having biases
4. Pigeonholing clients
5. Attending to facts
6. Rehearsing
7. Sympathizing
8. Interrupting

In the following sections of the chapter, we describe nonverbal and verbal ways to increase your attentiveness with clients.

The meanings people attach to different gestures or words have been learned. Some of the meanings are fairly standardized; others have distinct regional or cultural variances. For example, do you prefer to have people look at you when you talk to them? Most Americans do, but some Native Americans do not, and studies suggest that some inner-city African-American youths do not. When you are telling someone what you think, what would be your reaction if that person began to frown? If the frown was not consistent with your feelings, you probably would begin to question the inconsistency between your message and the listener's response. If you feel strongly about a topic and the other person does not seem to care about it, are you likely to continue telling the person about your feelings? No, since most of us want to know that our feelings are falling upon interested ears.

For these and many more reasons, your behavior can contribute to your client's feelings of security. This increased sense of security that occurs at the same time clients are talking about themselves can become a self-reinforcing phenomenon. Most of you have probably had the experience of entering a new activity and feeling nervous and unsure of yourselves. But as you stayed with the activity and nothing bad (perhaps even some good things) happened, before long, your self-confidence began to grow. So it is with counseling. As the client begins to experience your acceptance, your understanding, and your commitment, the feelings of vulnerability, uncertainty, caution, or lack of trust begin to dissipate. Is this a predictable reaction? Yes, it is, with the majority of clients who are in search of themselves, a better way to live life, or a better way to relate to others.

FACIAL EXPRESSIONS

Knapp has observed that the face is the "primary site for communication of emotional states; it reflects interpersonal attitudes; it provides nonverbal feedback on the comments of others; and some say it is the primary source of information next to human speech" (1978, p. 263). Facial expressions convey basic emotions such as anger, disgust, fear, sadness, and happiness. Unlike most other aspects of nonverbal attending behavior, facial expressions do not seem to vary much among cultures. These primary or basic emotions "seem to be represented by the same facial expressions across cultures, although individual cultural norms may influence how and when such emotions are expressed" (Harper, Wiens, & Matarazzo, 1978, p. 99). For example, anger is often conveyed cross-culturally through the eyes and by changes in the area of the mouth and jaw. However, men and women both within and between the same and different cultures may express anger in different ways and at different times. For instance, some persons may reject the idea of releasing anger because they have learned it is "unchristian" or "unladylike" (Kelley, 1979, p. 24).

Your facial expressions communicate messages to the client that are as meaningful as those you receive from the client's facial expressions. A primary, though often not intentional, way that counselors use their facial expressions is to reinforce client behavior. Perhaps it would be more accurate to say that the effect of your facial expressions is to reinforce, either positively or negatively, clients' verbal behavior. It is also important for your facial expressions to reflect those of the client—if the client expresses pleasure, you look happy; if the client conveys sadness, you show concern.

Animation

Animation in facial expression gives clients the feeling that you are alert and responding to ongoing communication. It may be that your facial expressions serve as a mirror for clients' feelings as well as an acceptance of them. Certainly, an absence of facial expressions (a deadpan look) will suggest a lack of interest, awareness, or mental presence to clients. The most noticeable expression is the smile. The appropriate use of smiles can have a powerful effect on clients, particularly when paired with occasional head nods. Continuous smiling, however, becomes a negative stimulus. Frequent frowns can communicate disapproval. Occasional frowns, on the other hand, communicate your failure to follow or understand a particular point and are therefore useful.

▲ EXERCISE 3.1: FACIAL EXPRESSIONS

A. Facial Attentiveness

With a partner, designate one of you as the speaker and the other as the listener. While the speaker shares one of his or her concerns, the listener's tasks are:

1. Do not respond with *any* facial expression or animation whatsoever while the speaker is talking; maintain complete facial passivity.
2. After two or three minutes, respond with a facial reaction that is opposite of the feelings and concerns being expressed by the speaker. For example, if the speaker is talking seriously, smile and look happy.
3. After another three minutes or so, respond with facial animation and expression that mirror the kind and intensity of feelings being expressed by the speaker.

Discuss the different results produced by these three approaches. Reverse roles and repeat the exercise. What can you conclude about facial attentiveness as a result of this exercise? What have you learned about yourself and your facial gestures? What do you want to change about your facial gestures and how do you intend to bring this change about?

B. Recognizing Facial Cues

Find two persons with whom to work. Designate one of you as the speaker for round 1; the second as the listener, and the third as the observer. Roles are rotated for round 2 and round 3. For each round, the listener feeds each of the four incomplete sentences to the speaker. The speaker repeats the sentence and adds the first completion that comes to his or her mind. The observer watches for changes and cues in the speaker's facial expressions as he or she works with all of the incomplete sentences in the round. For this to be most effective, when you are in the role of the speaker, take your time, breathe deeply, and say whatever comes into your mind without thinking about it or censoring it. The observer shares the observations with the speaker after the round is over.

1. Anger
   a. When I get angry . . . .
   b. I get angry when . . . .
   c. I feel disgusted that . . . .
   d. One thing that makes me mad is . . . .
2. Sadness
   a. When I get sad . . . .
   b. I get sad when . . . .
   c. I feel "blue" that . . . .
   d. One thing that makes me sad is . . . .
3. Fear
   a. When I get afraid . . . .
   b. I feel afraid that . . . .
   c. I get afraid when . . . .
   d. One thing that makes me afraid is . . . .

EYE CONTACT

What is the effect of eye contact? Research into interpersonal interaction indicates more than one effect. Knapp observes that eye contact "is frequently indicative of the nature of the relationship between the interactants" (1978, p. 132). It may signal a need for affiliation, involvement, or inclusion; it may reflect the quality of an existing relationship; or it may enhance the communication of a complex message. Eye contact can also produce anxiety in the other person. A gaze lasting longer than about 10 seconds can signal aggressiveness rather than acceptance.

Unlike facial expressions, eye contact patterns do vary among cultures. In Western culture, people emphasize the importance of maintaining eye contact while listening. In some cultures, an individual may look away as a sign of respect or may demonstrate more eye contact when talking and less eye contact while listening. Good eye contact—eye contact that reinforces clients and makes their communication easier—lies somewhere between the fixed gaze and "shifty eyes," or frequent breaks of eye contact. Look at clients when they are talking. Occasionally, permit your eyes to drift to an object away, *but not far away,* from the client. Then return your eyes to the client. Let yourself be natural. Do not be afraid to invite the client into the world of your vision.

▲ EXERCISE 3.2: EYE CONTACT

Perhaps you can better grasp the effects of eye contact by participating in the following dyadic exercise. With a partner, determine who will be the talker and who will be the listener. While the talker speaks, the listener should listen but avoid eye contact with the speaker. Then discuss the following questions: What are the effects on the speaker? How well did the speaker feel that he or she was able to communicate? Try the exercise again, but this time maintain eye contact with the speaker as described in the previous section. What effect does this have? Reverse roles and repeat the exercise.

BODY POSITIONS AND USE OF SPACE

Body positions serve important functions in a counseling session. Body positions and movement regulate space or distance between counselor and client, greeting of a client, termination of a session, and turn taking (that is, the exchange of speaker and listener roles within a conversation) (Cormier & Cormier, 1991, p. 93). Body movement and comfort with physical space (closeness or distance) vary among cultures and with gender. Generally in Western cultures, counselors and clients sit face to face. Even an intervening object such as a desk is often considered a distraction. Yet, as Ivey, Ivey, and Simek-Downing (1987, p. 53) noted, in some Eskimo and Inuit cultural groups, persons sit side by side when discussing a personal issue. Persons from Western cultures usually prefer several feet of distance between chairs; however, those from other cultures may be more comfortable with closer distances (Watson, 1970). The effects of space also vary with a client's expression of feelings. A client who has just expressed a lot of anger often requires more personal space than someone who is feeling sad or experiencing a lot of pain.

Gender also dictates what is considered appropriate space. Some females may be more comfortable with a closer distance to the counselor, especially if the counselor is female. However, many female clients may feel intruded upon if a male counselor positions himself too close for comfort. Clients with a history of severe physical and/or sexual abuse may require greater space, particularly at the beginning stage of counseling. To be respectful of clients, it is important to allow them to choose the appropriate amount of distance from the therapist in the counseling interactions.

One important aspect to body communication involves the amount of tension conveyed by the body. Astute counselors will note the degree of tension or relaxation in a client's body. A body that is blocking or holding back a feeling may be tense, with shallow, fast breathing. A relaxed body posture indicates comfort, both with the counseling setting and with the topic being discussed. Selective body tension communicates action. It may reflect a "working" moment for you—involvement with the client, movement toward a goal, or preparation for something new. Body tension that is continuous will probably communicate discomfort with the client, the topic, or yourself. To be comfortable with yourself, it is important to begin from a base of relaxation. The following exercises may help you to achieve a desired state of relaxation.

▲ EXERCISE 3.3: RELAXING

A. Muscle Relaxation

While sitting down, raise your hand and arms three to four inches above the armrests of the chair and then let them drop. Feel the tension flow out of your arms. Repeat this and try to increase the relaxation. Let your back and buttocks be in contact with as much of the chair as possible. Feel the chair pressing against your body. Tense the muscles in your legs and then release the tension. Feel the surge of warmth in your muscles as your legs relax. Repeat this tensing and releasing of leg muscles several times, each time achieving a little more relaxation. Now take three or four deep breaths slowly. After each breath, slowly release the air from your lungs. Do you feel more relaxed than when you started?

Do this exercise again, this time without any interruptions between different body exercises. This is a good exercise to do just before seeing a client. It is one of the ways by which you can prepare yourself for the session. As you do the exercise more often, you will find it easier and quicker to achieve a surprisingly comfortable state of relaxation.

B. Massage Relaxation

As you engage in this activity, breathe in and out through your nose in an even, balanced way. Rub the palms of your hands together for several minutes or until they feel very warm. Then lightly rest each hand on your head with your thumbs touching each temple. Place your hands on your forehead and smooth out any tension. Then gently massage this part of your head. Lightly massage over and under your eyes, moving your fingers down your nose as you massage under your eyes. Close your eyes and rest the palms of your hands on your eyes. Massage the area around your mouth and cheekbones. Move over to your jawbones and as you massage them open your mouth and move your jaws around. Next, take your fingertips and massage all around your ears, allowing sounds around you to soften as you do so. Work your hands around to the back of your neck and massage the tension accumulated in this area. When finished, take your hands and shake the tension out, away from your body. This activity can also be done with a partner.

Visible Behavior

Together, facial expressions, eye contact and body messages constitute the counselor's visible behavior. The impact of visible behavior on communication is considerable, as the following exercise will prove.

▲ EXERCISE 3.4: THE IMPACT OF VISIBLE BEHAVIOR

Egan (1976, p. 101) has described a simple exercise that illustrates the importance of what you see in another person when you communicate. This exercise will give you an opportunity to measure the effect of your facial and body gestures on the person receiving your message. Select as your partner a person you have been wanting to involve in a conversation. Sit down facing each other. Each of you close your eyes and keep them closed throughout the conversation. Talk to each other for about five minutes. Then open your eyes, complete the conversation, and discuss the differences between visual and nonvisual communication. What compensations did you have to make while talking without sight? How successful do you believe you were in your communication attempts? What, in particular, were you missing in terms of visual feedback from your partner?

VERBAL BEHAVIOR AND SELECTIVE ATTENTION

The things you say will have an immediate impact on your clients. Many studies have shown that the counselor's responses can mold and shape the direction of the client's responses. In other words, whatever topic you respond to with a verbal acknowledgment, the client will probably continue to talk about it. Topics that you do not respond to often get cut off or interrupted. This process is called *selective attention*. Ivey, Ivey, and Simek-Downing stated that "the pattern of selective attention may say more about the counselor than it does about the client. . . . Some counselors have clients who talk only about sex (or dreams or male-female relationships, or feminist concerns, etc.) while other counselors may have clients who never talk about sex" (1987, p. 54). Those authors also noted that it is important to be aware of your own patterns so that you do not inadvertently or unconsciously steer clients away from topics they need to discuss just because they are uncomfortable to you. If you become aware of this happening, it is useful to consult your supervisor (see also Chapter 11).

Several points should be considered in terms of your verbal impact. Fit your comments or questions into the context of the topic at hand. Do not interrupt clients or quickly change topics. Stay with the topics that clients introduce and help them develop and pursue them. This implies more than a technique; it is a highly conscious awareness of what is going on between you and your client. It is called *verbal following*. Practice verbal following in the following exercise.

▲ EXERCISE 3.5: VERBAL FOLLOWING

A. Roleplay of Verbal Following

In the roles of counselor and client, choose a partner and sit in pairs. Concentrate on using the verbal reinforcing behaviors discussed in this chapter. In your responses, react only to what the client has just said; do not add a new idea. Let your thinking be as close as possible to that of the client.

Prevent your facial gestures, body gestures, and verbal responses from distracting the client. After five minutes, stop the exercise and discuss with your client: What was your client most aware of in your behavior? How well did your client think you understood his or her communication? What, if any, behavior got in your client's way? Now reverse roles and repeat the exercise.

B. Verbal Following and Shifts in Focus

Below are some client statements followed by counselor responses. Describe each counselor response: Do you feel that it is a response to the client's statement? If not, describe the nature of the inappropriate response, such as *shift of topic, focus on others,* or *focus on past.*

  Client A: "I think I just have to go away for a while. The pressure is really building up.

  Counselor: "What would Bob say to that?" focused on other

The counselor did / did not (circle one) respond to the client's statement. If the counselor did not respond to the client's statement, the nature of the inappropriate response was ___focused on other___

> Client B: "She doesn't really care anymore, and I've got to learn to accept that."
>
> Counselor: "You are fairly sure that she doesn't care."

The counselor did / did not (circle one) respond to the client's statement. If the counselor did not respond to the client's statement, the nature of the inappropriate response was _____ .

> Client C: "Money is the biggest problem I have in school. The grades aren't that hard to get."
>
> Counselor: "What did you do last year?"

The counselor did / did not (circle one) respond to the client's statement. If the counselor did not respond to the client's statement, the nature of the inappropriate response was ___focused on the past___

> Client D: "The job I have isn't fun, but I'm afraid if I quit, I might not get another job."
>
> Counselor: "Jobs are really getting hard to find."

The counselor did / did not (circle one) respond to the client's statement. If the counselor did not respond to the client's statement, the nature of the inappropriate response was ___Shift the topic___

These exchanges illustrate some of the common pitfalls that await the counselor. In the exchange with client A, the response was probably inappropriate. The counselor seems to have jumped topics by bringing up Bob. In addition, the counselor ignored the client's reference to the pressure and its effect on him. The response given to client B could be quite appropriate, though it is not the only possible appropriate response. The counselor is responding directly to what the client said. The inappropriateness of the response to client C is more obvious, though no one would be surprised to hear the response if it were a social setting rather than a counseling setting. The counselor really did not respond to any of the key ideas in the client's statement (money, problem, or grades). Instead, the counselor decided, for some reason, to collect information about the client. Finally, the response to client D is also inappropriate. The client is talking about feelings ("isn't fun"; "afraid"). The counselor's response has nothing to do with the client.

Instead, the counselor shifted the focus to a social commentary on the current economic scene.

▲ EXERCISE 3.6: APPROPRIATE BEHAVIOR FOR COUNSELOR ATTENTIVENESS

Now that you are aware of behavioral descriptions of inappropriate social behaviors and attending behaviors in the counseling setting, can you deduce some appropriate behaviors? Be specific as to nonverbal components (face, eyes, tone of voice, rate of speech, etc.), body-language components (head, arms, body position, etc.), and verbal components (choice of words, types of responses, etc.). List them on a sheet of paper.

Discuss what you specified as appropriate counselor behaviors to enhance attentiveness. Try some out. You may find that you will need to eliminate some behaviors and relearn some others. This will take a little time and practice until you feel completely comfortable with your new styles. With a partner, decide which of the following appropriate counselor behaviors are not present in your current repertoire:

Facial animation
Good eye contact
Occasional head nodding
Soft, firm tone of voice
Occasional smiling
Occasional gesturing with hands
Moderate rate of speech
Response to primary stimulus of client communication
Verbal speech centers on client and on immediate present
Occasional use of minimal verbal reinforcers (e.g., "mm-hmm")

Set behavioral goals for yourself. What is it that you would like to be able to do as a result of your newly acquired learnings? Share this with your partner. Make some commitment about the kinds of things you are going to do this week to implement your goals. Your partner should do the same thing. This way you and your partner can give each other feedback about goal attainment as you continue to interact.

Vocal Characteristics

The use of a well-modulated, calm but energetic vocal tone and pitch will reassure clients of your own comfort with their problems. The use of intermittent one-word phrases (minimal verbal stimuli) serves much the same purpose as do head nods and eye contact. These are verbal signs that you are listening and following what the client is saying. The more common minimal verbal stimuli are "mm-hmm," "mmm," "ah," and so forth. There is one hazard that should be mentioned: Overuse of these vocal stimuli can produce a "parrotlike" effect that has negative results. Later chapters will describe how you can use minimal verbal stimuli and other types of reinforcing behaviors to assist clients in developing their thinking.

SUMMARY

One of the major goals in the counseling setting is to listen attentively and to communicate this attentiveness through the use of eye contact, intermittent head nods, a variety of facial expressions, relaxed posture, modulated voice, minimal verbal stimuli, and verbal components that follow the client's topics. The effect of this communication will be to reinforce verbal behavior, comfort, and clients' potential to examine and understand themselves.

DISCUSSION QUESTIONS

1. How much do you rely on reactions (gestures, verbal responses) from the other person when you are trying to communicate an important message?

2. What is your typical response when you feel that you are failing in your attempt to communicate with another person?

3. What goals or objectives have you set for yourself in terms of improving your ability to be a good listener? What do you plan to do to achieve these goals?

4. What are some additional examples for social behaviors that you would find distracting if you were involved in a sensitive discussion of your private life?

5. Recall an incident in which you were sharing a significant moment with another person and that person displayed some distracting behavior. What was the effect of that person's behavior on you? What did you decide was the reason for that person's behavior?

6. What do you notice about nonverbal behavior among persons from varying cultures?

RECOMMENDED READINGS

Cormier, W. H., & Cormier, L. S. (1991). *Interviewing strategies for helpers* (3rd ed.). Pacific Grove, CA: Brooks/Cole.

Chapter 4, "Nonverbal Behavior," provides a cogent summary of how counselor and client nonverbal behavior affects the counseling process.

Egan, G. (1990). *The skilled helper* (4th ed.) Pacific Grove, CA: Brooks/Cole.

Chapter 5, "Communication Skills 1: Attending and Listening," provides an excellent discussion of attentiveness, listening, and obstacles to this process.

Hermansson, G. L., Webster, A. C., & McFarland, K. (1988). Counselor deliberate postural lean and communication of facilitative conditions. *Journal of Counseling Psychology, 35,* 149–153.

This article describes the effects of counselor nonverbal facilitative conditions.

Ivey, A., Ivey, M., & Simek-Downing, L. (1987). *Counseling and psychotherapy* (2nd ed.). Englewood Cliffs, NJ: Prentice Hall.

Chapter 3, "The Skills of Intent and Interviewing," discusses the concepts and skills of attending behavior and selective attention.

Ivey, A., Ivey, M. B., & Simek-Morgan, L. (1993). *Counseling and psychotherapy: A multicultural perspective.* Boston: Allyn and Bacon.

Chapter 3, "Developing Intentional Interviewing Skills," discusses attentiveness skills from a multicultural perspective.

Johanson, G., & Kurtz, R. (1991). *Grace unfolding: Psychotherapy in the spirit of the Tao-te ching.* New York: Bell Tower, a division of Crown Publishers.

This is an eloquent and creative book in which the Eastern practice of mindfulness or centeredness, which corresponds to the concept of attending, is discussed with respect to clients as well as counselors.

Knapp, M. L. (1978). *Nonverbal communication in human interaction* (2nd ed.). New York: Holt, Rinehart & Winston.

Three chapters in this book are particularly relevant to the counselor: Chapter 4, "Effects of Physical Behavior on Human Communication"; Chapter 5, "Effects of the Face and Eyes on Human Communication"; and Chapter 6, "Effects of Vocal Cues which Accompany Spoken Words." Knapp has written a highly readable and interesting book that reflects research and its implications for communication.

Rogers, C. R. (1980). *A way of being.* Boston: Houghton Mifflin.

Rogers discusses attentiveness as a way of participating in a human partnership with the client.

▶ 4

Recognizing Communication Patterns

We have shown how verbal and nonverbal behaviors are the means by which core conditions such as empathy and warmth are communicated. The next level in this very complicated process involves the communication patterns that emerge as the counselor-client relationship develops. Issues related to the locus of control and responsibility in the session, choice of topics, timing, and other therapeutic logistics are undefined at the outset of counseling. In the first few sessions, these issues are resolved, either openly or tacitly, and become apparent through understanding the communication patterns that evolve.

There are many ways to think about patterning in the counseling process. Some patterning takes the form of ritual, whereas other patterning is responsive. That is to say, some of the behaviors become ritualized as a function of routine; for example, the client always chooses the chair facing the window, the counselor always begins by asking, "What is on your mind today?" and so forth. Other patterns are negotiations between counselor and client, the intent of which may be to settle such matters as, "Are we really going to work today?" or "I want you to take charge because I'm feeling overwhelmed." An example of this has been provided in a study by Friedlander and Phillips (1984), who found that frequent topic shifts (or changes) in the early sessions were an indication that a struggle for control over the process was being waged between counselor and client. If such a struggle was going on and the counselor was unaware of it, the implications for progress would be questionable.

RITUALIZED PATTERNS OF COMMUNICATION

Ritualized patterns may be either situation specific or idiosyncratic to the individuals involved. We have already mentioned examples of situation-specific patterning with the client who always chooses a certain chair to sit in. This act of repeated choice may arise out of a very simple condition. It was the chair selected by the client at the initial session, and its continued selection in subsequent sessions offers familiar ground and reflects that the client feels no need to make a different choice. However, if the client arrives for the fifth session and, with no explanation, chooses a different chair, the act of choice may contain unspecified meaning. In other words, through the act of choosing, something is communicated, but what is communicated is unclear until the counselor questions the client.

Ritualized Counselor Patterns

The same situation may apply to the counselor. Most experienced counselors develop a style of interaction with their clients. Although their style takes individuals into account, it is nonetheless patterned and, as such, is a kind of trademark of that counselor's work. For example, a counselor may use the first several minutes of the session as relationship time and may communicate this to clients. Or a different counselor may view the first few minutes as history-taking time. However, should a client arrive in a distraught state, that pattern may be suspended and therapeutic work may begin immediately.

Ritualized Client Patterns

Clients also become involved in ritualized patterns of communication. Often these patterns evolve out of assumptions about what the counselor wants or expects from the client. For example, a client may assume that the counselor expects to hear an account of the week's worries. The fact that this happened in the second session had led the client to think such an account is expected, and so he or she continues the practice in subsequent sessions. Thus, although the activity has little or nothing to do with the process, it remains a part of the pattern.

INTERACTIVE COMMUNICATION PATTERNS

Most patterning, and certainly the most significant patterning that occurs in the counseling session, is interactive in nature. It has been suggested by Cormier and Hackney (1992) that most clients approach counseling with two conflicting motivations: (1) "I know I need help" and (2) "I wish I weren't here." Given this dual set of motivations, the client may be expected to convey conflicting and even contradictory communications at times. Similarly, counselors must resolve the potential conflict that was mentioned in Chapter 2 regarding unconditional positive regard and congruence (Lietaer, 1984). We mention these conflicting tendencies because they can confuse the communication process. It is essential that the counselor know his or her inner motivations and conflicts. In addition to these inner motivations, interactive communication patterns are also influenced by culture and gender.

Communication and Culture

Many communication patterns are affected by both cultural heritage and gender. Sue provided a cogent discussion of how communication patterns can be affected in culturally different ways. He observed that "in traditional Japanese culture, children have been taught not to speak until addressed. Patterns of communication tend to be vertical, flowing from those of higher prestige and status to those of lower prestige and status. Likewise, there are many cultural groups in which restraint of strong feelings is highly valued. It is equated with wisdom and maturity" (1992, p. 12). Unfortunately, a culturally uninformed counselor may view varying patterns of client communication such as the above in pejorative ways. For example, a client practicing restraint may be viewed by a culturally uninformed counselor as being "inarticulate, less intelligent, inhibited, lacking in spontaneity, or repressed" (Sue, 1992).

Communication and Gender

Communication patterns are also influenced by gender (Tannen, 1990). Tannen has described patterns of communication among women as "rapport talk" and among men as "report talk" (Simpkinson & Simpkinson, 1992). In rapport talk, women talk easily about private, intimate topics and about feelings. They talk to create a connection. In report talk, men discuss facts, figures, and share information. They talk to make a point or establish a position. Women tend to be more nonconfrontational in communication with others. They also are often more comfortable in disclosing concerns and troubles and asking for help. Men are often more reticent to request help and place more emphasis on solutions or "fixing" problems.

Tannen (1990) has stated that observation of such gender differences in language and style of communication helps both genders to be more accepting and respectful of differences. Since style is a learned and somewhat automatic process, awareness of our own style also may help us develop greater flexibility in responding to clients.

▲ EXERCISE 4.1: COMMUNICATION PATTERNS

A. Cultural Differences

In a small group, discuss ways in which communication patterns may vary among cultures. Relate your observations to the counseling process.

B. Gender Differences

Observe the way men and women talk, even in ordinary, noncounseling conversations. What similarities and differences do you note? How do you think these similarities and differences will affect the counseling situation?

SILENCE

For most beginning counselors, silence can be frightening. It seems to bring the total focus of attention on them, revealing their most glaring weaknesses as counselors—at least this is how many beginning counselors describe their experiences with silence. As a result, their tendency is to say something—anything—to prevent silence. Typically, a question is asked. Often it is a bad question—one that can be answered by a minimal response from the client. The answer to the question is relatively unimportant, since the question was not well thought out by the counselor. The counselor may not even be listening to the answer. Such a state of affairs suggests that it is the counselor's responsibility to keep the client talking, that talking is the only evidence that the client is working, and that silence is probably non-therapeutic or a waste of time. None of these assumptions is valid. As Karasu has noted, the importance of silence is frequently overlooked, as "therapists tend to underestimate the power of listening and overestimate the power of speaking" (1992, pp. 81–82).

Silence has a similar effect on clients. They also perceive silence as a demanding condition and feel a need to fill the gaps of silence with talking. Because clients react to silence in this way, you can use silence as a counseling technique and as a way of responding to clients. Silence has another meaning that is important to acknowledge. After a period of hard work in the session, or after a moment of significant insight, the client often needs time to absorb the experience, to fit it into his or her existing system.

This results in an *integration silence,* one in which the client is experiencing fully the therapeutic moment. You may not encounter this in your first counseling sessions, but you will as you gain experience.

Types of Silence

Silence can be a therapeutic moment as well as a self-conscious moment. What makes one silence different from another? What are the dimensions of silence in a counseling session? Silence can be categorized broadly as counselor induced or client induced. Counselor-induced silence occurs at a time when the focus of the interview is on the counselor. In other words, if the counselor, rather than the client, is feeling responsible for the moment and responds with silence, that is a counselor-induced silence. Conversely, if the client has been talking, assuming responsibility, and then stops, that is a client-induced silence.

Counselor-Induced Silence

Counselor-induced silence can be examined in two contexts: the counselor's intentions and the consequences of the silence. Counselor intentions can vary widely. The underparticipatory counselor gives very little verbally. It is a style of behavior that may reflect the counselor's interpersonal interactions with people in general. It does not reflect therapeutic intentions. Rather, it may indicate a generalized tendency to hide, to withhold, to protect oneself from other people.

A second form of silence is that which occurs unsystematically. It is like being at a loss for words. Its intention is probably to give the counselor time to absorb and comprehend all that is going on at the moment. Again, it is not intended by the counselor to be a therapeutic moment, though the effect is often therapeutic. Many times a counselor will fail to respond to the moment, for personal reasons, and the effect is to encourage the client to continue more deeply into the topic or the feeling. When this happens, the counselor is more apt to feel lucky rather than competent.

The third form of counselor-induced silence is that which the counselor has deliberately presented. It may be that the counselor has been very active and has decided to reduce that activity, thus transferring more responsibility to the client. Or it may be that the counselor senses a momentum on the client's part that will lead to insight, commitment, or new relevant issues. In this case, the counselor chooses not to respond, in order not to interfere with or impede the client's psychological momentum.

Client-Induced Silence

Client-induced silence also has varied intentions and consequences. As noted with counselor silence, client silence is affected by the issue of responsibility and what to do with it. If the client is feeling irresponsible or underresponsible, the intention behind the silence may be antitherapeutic or antigrowth. For example, suppose Betty has developed a life pattern of avoiding some personal issues. When these issues arise, her natural response is to deny or ignore them by deflecting attention from herself. In the counseling setting, she may be aware that these personal issues are the source of her difficulties. Yet her natural reaction continues to be avoidance, deflection, or resistance. In this example, Betty's silence would reflect an attempt to transfer momentary responsibility to the counselor and away from herself. If she is successful, the consequence would be yet another time when important issues are avoided and underresponsibility is rewarded.

Another reason clients lapse into silence is to try to catch up on the progress of the moment. Counseling sessions sometimes move very quickly, covering a lot of ground, incorporating and relating many issues to one another. There is a need to stop, catch one's breath, observe the progress, or comprehend the implications. This is a very therapeutic type of silence. It allows clients to fit the new growth or insight that has occurred into their existing system. In effect, the client alters the existing system to include what has just been learned. There are also times when client-induced silence results from clients' opening some new doors to their awareness. For instance, Robert, who with his wife, Carolyn, had been in counseling for several weeks, lapsed into a silence during a discussion of "families of origin" (a technique used to identify styles, expectations, rules of interpersonal living). After a silence of a minute or more, he stated to the therapist and his wife, "I've been living with Carolyn for six years and thinking that I was overcoming the life I had with my parents. Now I can see that I have been more a reflection of my parents' home than I realized. I wonder what I really do believe in and want from my own family."

Silence also has different meanings from one culture to another. According to Sue and Sue (1977), in some cultures, silence does not mean that the client wants to stop talking but rather wishes to convey respect. Patterns of silence may also vary with gender. A woman may wait for a pause in the conversation to make a point; a man may interrupt a conversation to offer a fact. When expressing feelings, a woman may do so with great verbal facility; a man may pause frequently or present his feelings more hesitantly (Simpkinson & Simpkinson, 1992, p. 30).

How are you to know what kind of silence is occurring? The intention of a client-induced silence must always be inferred. By watching the client closely and by being sensitive to the themes, the issues, and the feelings being expressed, you will be gathering clues to what is happening. Is the client relaxed? Are the client's eyes fixed on something without being focused? This may mean the client is thinking about or pondering something or examining a new idea, or ruminating around in his or her mind. Or is the client tense, appearing nervous, looking from one object to another and avoiding eye contact? If so, this may mean that he or she is avoiding some topic or idea.

Therapeutic Silence

Skilled counselors often use silence as their best technique for specific situations. This does not suggest that they are inactive. There is always nonverbal behavior that adds meaning to the silence, thereby communicating a therapeutic message to the client. The messages that the counselor may seek to communicate include "I want us to move a bit more slowly"; "I want you to think more about what you just said"; "I don't accept the message you just presented"; or "I care very much about you and your feelings in this moment." There are other therapeutic messages that can be communicated through silence, but these tend to be the most common.

Pacing the Interview

Counseling interviews can be compared to a musical score. They have variations in theme, timing, activity, and inactivity. As you acquire self-comfort and skills, you will become aware that the different times in an interview have very different qualities. The counselor is a conductor of sorts for this therapeutic score. There are times when the client is hyperactive, babbling, or overacting, and the desired objective is to slow down the pace of the session. You can always verbally call attention to the client's activity; oftentimes silence achieves the same objective. You may not respond with total silence. Occasional verbal responses let the client know that you are still a participant. But you may want to monitor your reactions and not respond to all that stimulates you.

The use of silence to pace the session is especially important in initial interviews when the conditions of trust and safety are being built. Especially in these sessions, it is important to let the client determine the pace. As Hutchins and Cole noted, "The helping interview may be one of the few opportunities the client has to fully express thoughts and feelings without being rushed or pressed to perform. This luxury of unhurried time allows more complete expression than is typical in most clients' interactions" (1992, p. 95).

Silent Focusing

One of the ways in which silence is most useful is to focus attention on the moment. It is like stopping to listen to an echo. Throughout the book we will be suggesting ways in which you can help clients hear themselves. Silence is the first of these ways. Sometimes clients make totally irrational statements. By not responding to the statement, you allow the client messages to remain present, to continue to be heard even by the clients themselves. Or clients may make a statement of such relevance that you want to give them time to absorb the impact of that relevance. This would be the case when a client has just acknowledged a significant insight and needs time to fit this insight into an existing system of meanings.

Responding to Defenses

Occasionally, clients come to the interview filled with emotions that belong to other people or situations, yet they spill them out on you or the counseling process. Or you may make a statement to which the client responds defensively. These situations often reflect a lack of client awareness, though they are moments when the potential for awareness is great. The temptation for you may be to give the client insight into the situation. Often it is more meaningful to allow clients to give themselves that insight. This can be done by using silence as your response.

Silent Caring

Silent caring occurs in those moments when no words are an adequate response to the feelings that are present. It may be a moment of quiet weeping for the client, or it may be a moment of heavy melancholy. Whatever the feeling may be, it is one of those moments when experiencing the feeling fully is more important than making it go away. You can communicate your compassion and involvement very clearly with caring silence.

▲ EXERCISE 4.2: BEING COMFORTABLE WITH SILENCE

In our culture, people often have to learn to be silent. Perhaps you find silence to be intense and uncomfortable. If so, this exercise will help you become more comfortable with silence. Team up with two other people. One person will be the talker, you be the listener, and the third person can be the timekeeper. Invite the talker to talk about anything he or she wishes. You will listen and respond. But, before you respond, allow a pause to occur. Begin with 5-second pauses. Gradually increase the duration of pauses until you are allowing 15 seconds to pass before responding. The timekeeper should sit in a position from which he or she can signal the number of seconds to you without distracting the talker. After a 10-minute discussion, rotate roles and repeat the exercise until all three of you have had a turn as listener.

As a variation on this exercise, consider your contacts with people you encounter every day. Become conscious of your interaction patterns. Do you interject your reactions as soon as the other person has completed a communication? Do you interrupt the other person, thus preventing the slightest possibility of a silence? During the next few days, monitor your response behavior. When someone speaks to you, pause and think about the message for a few seconds and then give your response. Record any feedback you receive from your friends or acquaintances regarding your communication behavior.

SUMMARY

The practice of professional counseling involves a compromise between personal authenticity and professional skills. Both authenticity and skills are maintained by patterns of behavior that emerge as the counselor matures and grows in experience. Similarly, clients evolve patterns of behavior that reflect both their personal qualities and their problems. We have noted how these patterns affect and are affected by the counselor's interventions.

The beginning counselor's most noticeable patterns are those involving interactive qualities as well as cultural and gender factors. As the counselor's comfort level with the counseling setting improves, these patterns may be examined for their effect on the session. More subtle, and perhaps of greater concern, are the counselor patterns that become ritualized. Ritualized patterns exist for expediency's sake. They are the behavioral shorthand that allows more efficient functioning. The problem is that efficient functioning may not be effective functioning, particularly in the helping relationship. Consequently, it is professionally imperative that counselors examine their patterns of interaction with clients, not just early in their careers but throughout their careers.

DISCUSSION QUESTIONS

1. If you are able to eliminate inappropriate social behavior from your counseling repertoire, what impression do you think this will make on your client?

2. What types of messages can be communicated with a silence? How many of these messages might occur in a counseling session? How can you tell one message from another?

3. What do you think your own tolerance/comfort level is with silence? Are you more comfortable with silence that is initialed by you or the client?

4. Discuss some examples in which you have observed communication patterns being influenced by culture.

5. Describe your reactions to the idea that gender affects communications.

RECOMMENDED READINGS

Hutchins, P., & Cole, C. (1992). *Helping relationships and strategies* (2nd ed.). Pacific Grove, CA: Wadsworth, Brooks/Cole.

Chapter 8, "The Effective Use of Silence," is especially pertinent to the discussion of this important facet of the counseling process.

Karasu, T. (1992). *Wisdom in the practice of psychotherapy.* New York: Basic Books.

Karasu discusses a number of factors that influence the use of silence in the therapeutic process.

Pedersen, P. (1991). Multiculturism as a fourth force in counseling. *The Journal of Counseling and Development, 70,* 4–250.

This entire issue focuses on a variety of multicultural issues in counseling, including direct service delivery and conceptual issues.

Scher, M., & Good, G. (1990). Gender issues in counseling. *The Journal of Counseling and Development, 68,* 370–391.

These feature articles include a discussion of gender issues in counseling, gender roles, and gender-aware therapy.

Simpkinson, A., & Simpkinson, C. (1992, January/February). Man talk/woman talk. *Common Boundary,* 30–33.

This article succinctly describes some differences in communication patterns of women and men based upon a dialogue between Deborah Tannen and Robert Bly.

Sue, D. W. (1992). The challenge of multiculturalism: The road less traveled. *American Counselor, 1,* 6–15.

In this challenging article about multiculturalism, Sue discusses how cultural heritage affects the communication process in counseling.

Tannen, D. (1990). *You just don't understand.* New York: Basic Books.

Tannen discusses her research on gender differences in communication and conversation.

▶ 5

Managing the Counseling Session

We have discussed the qualities of a therapeutic relationship and how effective counselors attend to and understand the client. But we have not yet discussed the *structure* within which all this occurs. Experienced counselors enter each session with a sense of who they are, what they wish to do (or to be) in the session, and how they will represent themselves to the client. This is true in the first session as well as the twentieth session. As we mentioned in the previous chapter, experienced counselors develop a personal style that they carry into the relationship. That style provides the structure, the directions for how to begin the process—how to develop it and how to end or terminate it.

In this chapter we shall consider some awkward and sensitive times in the counseling relationship that require structure. Many counselors and clients have difficulty with beginnings and endings, whether they be the beginning or ending of a counseling interview or the beginning or ending of a counseling relationship. As you read the chapter, you will find suggestions and thoughts that may help you make smoother transitions into and out of these moments. There are two types of beginnings that will be examined: beginning the first interview you have with a client and beginning subsequent interviews. Similarly, we examine the two types of termination: session termination and relationship termination.

THE FIRST INTERVIEW

Your first interview with a client will have a special set of dynamics operating. It is the beginning of a potentially significant relationship. As

such, there are hopes and expectations, fears and reservations, acute awareness of some conditions and an amazing lack of awareness of other conditions—all of which have a bearing on the session. With so many emotional
issues operating, you might be wondering how you can possibly have a
successful first interview. Counselors deal with this issue in one of two
ways. Some counselors choose to work with the relationship dynamics that
are operating. Others choose to make the first session an intake interview
and collect needed information about the client. Whichever choice you
make, you must still attend to the other issue later. If you focus on interpersonal dynamics in the first session, in the second or third interview you will
want to collect information. If you use the first session as an intake session,
soon afterward you must begin to acknowledge relationship dynamics.

If you wish to focus on relationship dynamics, then the content of
Chapter 2 is particularly relevant. Specifically, you will want to achieve an
accurate sense of the client's world and communicate that understanding
back to your client. Learning to understand means putting aside your own
agenda long enough to allow the client's world to enter your awareness. It
means not worrying about yourself ("Am I doing the right thing?" "Am I
looking nervous?" etc.). Until you have had the experience of several
beginning sessions, this will be a difficult task. Of course, you will have an
underlying set of objectives in this session:

1. To reduce your client's initial anxieties to a level that permits him or her
   to begin talking
2. To refrain from excessive talking, since that takes time away from your
   client
3. To listen carefully to what your client is saying and attempt to recon-
   struct in your thinking the world that he or she is describing
4. To be aware that your client's choice of topics gives insight into his or
   her priorities for the moment

Initial Moments

In addition to these objectives, there are some logistics that require your
attention. In opening the interview, be on time. This communicates respect.
The beginning point can be as simple as a smile from you, along with a
simple introduction and a motion to show the client where to sit. For
example:

"Hello, I'm Bill Janutolo. Please have a seat here, or in that chair, if
you wish."

After introductions, you might allow a brief pause to occur. This gives your client a chance to talk if he or she is prepared to begin. Or you might proceed to give the first interview some structure. There are questions that must be resolved. How long will the interview be? How do you want your client to address you? What should your client expect the sessions to be like? What are your client's rights? What will be your role? Answers to these and other questions provide the structure for the relationship.

Structuring has been defined as the way the counselor defines the nature, limits, roles, and goals within the counseling relationship (Brammer, Shostrom, & Abrego, 1989). It includes comments about time limits, number of sessions, confidentiality, possibilities and expectations, as well as observation and/or tape-recording procedures. Describing the counseling process and providing structure reduces the unknowns and thus reduces the anxiety of clients. It also permits clients the opportunity to check out their expectations. Kottler summarized the ingredients of effective structuring in initial sessions as follows:

1. Providing a general overview and preview of the counseling process
2. Assessing the client's expectations and promoting positive ones
3. Describing the counselor's expectations
4. Orienting the client to new language and new behaviors
5. Helping the client to increase tolerance for frustration and discomfort
6. Obtaining client commitment (1991, pp. 141–144)

Confidentiality

You will want to emphasize the issue of confidentiality to new clients. Does it mean you will talk to no one? What are the implications if you are being observed by a supervisor or if you are tape-recording the session? Will you keep a written record? If so, what are the client's guarantees that the record will be kept confidential? Some of these may not be relevant issues, in which case it would be better not to introduce them as issues. You can discuss this with a colleague or supervisor to determine which issues are relevant and which are not. Here is how one counselor begins a session with structuring:

We have about an hour together. I like to tape-record interviews with my clients. It's easier and less interfering than taking notes. I hope that won't bother you. I'm not sure what brings you here, but whatever it is that is bothering you will be treated in strict confidentiality. You can talk about anything you wish.

Exceptions to Confidentiality

According to ethical guidelines for helping professions, the counselor is generally obligated to treat the client's communication in a confidential manner; that is, the counselor agrees to not share information given by the client with other persons. However, there are several exceptions to this general policy, such as when the client's condition indicates harm to self or others (American Counseling Association, 1981). Some states also have legal statutes that require helpers to report instances of child abuse or to testify under subpoena. The important point is to discuss with clients both the protection and the limits of confidentiality as a part of the structuring process.

Encouraging the Client to Talk

After providing this initial structure, you and your client are ready to begin work. The obvious beginning is to get your client to talk, to indicate his or her reason for entering counseling, and perhaps to indicate in some form what he or she hopes to achieve as a result of counseling (the client's first statement of counseling goals). Your beginning will be an invitation to the client to talk. The nature of this invitation is important. A good invitation is one that encourages but does not specify what the client should talk about. This is called an *unstructured invitation* or an *open-ended lead*.

Unstructured Invitations

The unstructured invitation has two purposes:

1. It gives the client an opportunity to talk.
2. It prevents the counselor from identifying the topic the client should discuss.

An unstructured invitation is a statement in which the counselor encourages clients to begin talking about whatever is of concern to them. For example:

"Please feel free to go ahead and begin."
"Where would you like to begin today?"
"You can talk about whatever you would like."
"Perhaps there is something particular you want to discuss."
"What brings you to counseling?"

By contrast, a structured invitation—one that specifies a topic—gives clients little room to reflect on the motives, goals, or needs that brought them to counseling. An example of a less desirable structured invitation to talk might be: "Tell me about what careers you are considering." The client is obviously tied down to a discussion of careers by this invitation, thus delaying or even negating a more relevant issue. *(Note:* If careers are what the client wants to discuss, an unstructured invitation allows this topic to emerge as well as a structured invitation would.)

The following exercise will help you develop the skills involved in initiating the interview.

▲ EXERCISE 5.1: INITIATING AN INTERVIEW

This is a class exercise that requires a videotape system. Have class members select partners. Each pair is to decide who is to be the interviewer and who is to be interviewed. The exercise is to last for five minutes. The interviewer is to work toward achieving the following goals:

1. Set the interviewee at ease (body relaxed, voice without tension).
2. Set the interviewer at ease (body less tense, open posture).
3. Get the interviewee to start talking about anything (use unstructured invitation, silence).
4. Get the interviewee to *identify* a current concern (acknowledge that the client came to counseling for a reason; ask about reason).

Following each exercise, reverse roles and repeat the procedure. Then, when all pairs have had the opportunity to do the exercise, replay the tape and discuss the encounters, using the following format:

1. Ask the interviewer's reaction to the tape.
2. Describe those behaviors that were good in the exercise.
3. Identify and describe those elements in which there is room for further growth.

OBJECTIVES OF THE FIRST INTERVIEW

If your objective in the first interview is to focus on client feelings or interpersonal dynamics, you will find yourself using responses that elicit feelings, describe relationships, and communicate your understanding. These responses include restatement, reflection of feeling, summarization of feelings, requests for clarification, and acknowledgment of nonverbal behavior. These types of response encourage the client to present and explore thoughts and feelings, and give you an opportunity to understand some of the unique perceptions your clients may have.

On the other hand, you may wish to use the first interview to collect as much information as possible about your client, and not become involved with intrapersonal dynamics. This approach characterizes the intake interview and is based on the rationale that the more you know about the client's world, the better you are able to understand and respond to intrapersonal dynamics, particularly those perceptions that may be slightly distorted. An intake interview is highly structured. There are specific topics you want the client to discuss. The types of response that you will use in this interview tend to be probes, accents, closed questions, and requests for clarification, although the other mentioned responses may also be used on occasion.

COUNSELOR RESPONSES THAT ENCOURAGE CLIENT EXPRESSION

We have already described the unstructured invitation as a response to encourage the client to begin talking. It remains for us to describe the other responses that can be used in the initial interview, depending on your purpose in that session. These responses are also used in subsequent counseling sessions and will be reintroduced in later chapters that describe specific objectives. First, let us consider those responses that are most useful when you focus on feeling and dynamics.

Restatement

Although it is important to maintain a listening role, there are certain kinds of responses that communicate not only that you are listening but also that you are a person with an active role. The *restatement* is one of these responses. It is a verbatim repetition of the main thought or feeling expressed by your client's preceding communication. An example is the following interaction:

> Client: "I don't know whether to stay in school or to drop out and get a job. But if I did drop out, I don't know what kind of job I could find."
> Counselor: "You don't know whether to stay in school or to drop out."

In this example, the client has communicated two thoughts: whether to stay in school and uncertainty about finding a job. When the counselor uses a restatement, it is easy to respond to the last thought emitted by the client, since it is the most immediate communication. However, this is a poor criterion. It is better to pick out the primary thought or feeling of the client's communication, regardless of its position in the statement. Just as a caution, it should be noted that the overuse of restatements produces a "parrotlike" effect in the interview. As a guide, the restatement can be used no more than about once or twice per topic without producing this mimic effect.

Reflection of Feeling

The *reflection of feeling* is a paraphrased response to a feeling communicated by the client, either verbally or nonverbally. The statement accomplishes precisely what its name implies: a mirroring of the feelings or emotion present in the client's message. Chapter 7 explores the different levels that this type of response can reflect. For our purposes in opening an interview, the following examples are sufficient.

Reflection of a verbally expressed feeling:

> *Client:*   "One of my main problems is that I need to come out of myself. And, uh, when I'm with people, or even when I'm alone, I have a loss for words. I have nothing to say; you know."
>
> *Counselor:*   "So when you are with other people, it must be a feeling like there's nothing inside you to come out and be noticed."

Reflection of a nonverbally expressed feeling:

> *Client:*   (Sitting in chair in slumped position, eyes downcast, forlorn look on face.)
>
> *Counselor:*   "From the way you look, you must be feeling pretty alone, pretty wiped out right now."

Summarization of Feeling

The summarization-of-feeling response is similar to the reflection of feeling, with one exception: It represents a set of feelings that might have been communicated over a period of minutes in the interview. Again, it is a paraphrase by the counselor that pulls together several feelings.

> *Client:*   "And that gets very uncomfortable, you know, with people. With a big group I'm fine, listening . . . or if I have something to say I get it out, usually. Usually, it takes me a very long

time, and when I do come out, you see, I consider it's not worth saying and half the time, I think, I don't come out with it. Um . . . and that gets uncomfortable. And then I get the feeling like when I'm with people that if I can't be rambling off an awful lot of information, you know, then I'm not worth anything, you know? And that kind of thing bothers me."

Counselor: "Let me see if I understand all of that. In large groups you can feel a little safer sometimes if nobody notices you, but if you have something you want to say, it is so hard finding a way to say it that you finally decide it's probably not worth hearing if it's that hard to say. And that gets you to feeling down on yourself again."

Request for Clarification

Sometimes client responses sound cryptic or confused, and you are left wondering just what the client was trying to say. It can be very important to seek clarification in these moments rather than guessing or assuming that the communication was unimportant. The request for clarification asks the client to rephrase the communication. It can be stated in several ways:

"Could you try to describe that feeling in another way? I'm not sure I am following what you mean."

"When you say 'fuzzy,' what's that feeling like?"

"I think I got lost in that. Could you go through the sequence of events again for me?"

Acknowledgment of Nonverbal Behavior

The nonverbal-behavior acknowledgment is a response that speaks to an obvious client gesture or posture without interpreting the meaning of the behavior. In this way, this response is different from the reflection of non-verbally expressed feeling. Although it is important that you resist any inclination to interpret the client's behavior verbally, you may speculate or ask for clarification of the nonverbal gesture. If the behavior has meaning, your client can tell you what the meaning is. Examples of acknowledgment of nonverbal behavior include the following:

"You are holding your body really tight right now."

"You look quizzical. Do you follow what I am saying?"

"Your body is looking more relaxed now. Are you feeling more relaxed?"

COUNSELOR RESPONSES THAT SOLICIT INFORMATION

Since the intake interview is intended primarily to solicit information, the types of responses that characterize it include, but are not restricted to, those that follow.

Open-Ended Questions

Open-ended questions require more than a minimal or one-word response by the client. This type of question is introduced with either *what*, *where*, *when* or *how*. You will find that it is very difficult to ask questions that clearly place the focus on your client. Fairly often, it happens that counselors ask questions that allow the client to respond with either a yes or a no. The result is that the client assumes no responsibility for the content of the interview. The purpose of the open question is to prevent this from happening. The following questions are examples of open-ended questions:

"What are you thinking when you are silent?"
"How do you plan to find employment?"
"When do you feel anxious?"

The Accent

The accent is a one- or two-word restatement that focuses or brings attention to a preceding client response. It is said in a tone of voice that suggests that the counselor would like the client to elaborate. For example:

Client: "I'd like to have more self-confidence, but then I'd only be fooling myself."
Counselor: "Fooling yourself?"

Client: "After I returned from the meeting. I really felt dragged out."
Counselor: "Dragged out?"

The Closed Question

When your objective is to get the client to talk about anything, the closed question is not a good response. However, when you want the client to give a specific piece of information, it can be the best response available. For example:

"How old were you when your parents died?"
"How many brothers and sisters do you have?"

"What medication are you taking now?"

"Have you ever received counseling or therapy?"

The Request for Clarification

Requests for clarification can be used for soliciting information as well as for encouraging the client to elaborate about his or her feelings. It is important to keep in mind that such requests can be overused or underused. When overused, they can become distractors that repeatedly interrupt the client's train of thought. When they are underused, however, the counselor may have difficulty understanding what the client is saying. Sometimes the counselor is reluctant to seek clarification lest it impede or distract the client from the topic. If you are simply unable to follow the client's train of thought, it is more important to seek clarification than it is to allow the client to proceed. For example:

"Could you go over that again for me?"

"Could you explain that relationship to me again?"

"What did you mean a while ago when you said your parents were pretty indifferent?"

INTAKE-INTERVIEW CONTENT

We have repeatedly described the intake as an information-gathering interview, but we have not indicated what that information should be. This section presents a suggested outline of topics to cover and the rationale for their importance.

An assumption behind the intake interview is that the client is coming to counseling for more than one interview and intends to address problems or concerns that involve other people, other settings, and the future, as well as the present. Most counselors try to limit intake interviews to an hour. In order to do this, you must assume responsibility and control over the interview. The following is a suggested outline to follow:

I. Identifying Data

    A. Client's name, address, telephone number through which client can be reached. This information is important in the event the counselor needs to contact the client between sessions. The client's address also gives some hint about the conditions under which the client lives (large apartment complex, student dormitory, private home, etc.).

B. Age, sex, ethnic origin, marital status, occupational and educational status. Again, this is information that can be important. It lets you know when the client is still legally a minor and provides a basis for understanding information that will come out in later sessions.

II. Presenting Problems, Both Primary and Secondary

It is best when these are presented in exactly the way the client reported them. If the problem has behavioral components, these should be recorded as well. The following questions can help reveal this type of information:

A. How much does the problem interfere with the client's everyday functioning?

B. How does the problem manifest itself? What are the thoughts, feelings, and so on that are associated with it? What observable behavior is associated with it?

C. How often does the problem arise? How long has the problem existed?

D. Can the client identify a pattern of events that surround the problem? When does it occur? With whom? What happens before and after its occurrence?

E. What caused the client to decide to enter counseling at this time?

III. Client's Current Life Setting

How does the client spend a typical day or week? What social and religious activities, recreational activities, and so on are present? What is the nature of the client's vocational and/or educational situation? What is the client's living environment like? What are the client's most important current relationships?

IV. Family History

A. Father's and mother's ages, occupations, descriptions of their personalities, relationships of each to the other and each to the client and other siblings.

B. Names, ages, and order of brothers and sisters; relationship between client and siblings.

C. Is there any history of emotional disturbance and/or substance abuse in the family?

D. Descriptions of family stability, including number of jobs held, number of family moves, significant losses, and so on. This information provides insights in later sessions when issues related to client stability and/or relationships emerge.

V. Personal History

A. Medical history: any unusual or relevant illness or injury from prenatal period to present, including hospitalizations, surgeries, or substance abuse.

    B. Educational history: academic progress through grade school, high school, and post-high school. This includes extracurricular interests and relationships with peers.

    C. Military service record.

    D. Vocational history: Where has the client worked, at what types of jobs, for what duration, and what were the relationships with fellow workers?

    E. Sexual and marital history: Where did the client receive sexual information? What was the client's dating history? Any engagements and/or marriages? Other serious emotional involvements prior to the present? Reasons that previous relationships terminated? What was the courtship like with present spouse? What were the reasons (spouse's characteristics, personal thoughts) that led to marriage? What has been the relationship with spouse since marriage? Are there any children? Separations? Divorces?

    F. What experience has the client had with counseling and what were the client's reactions? Who referred the client?

    G. What are the client's personal goals in life?

VI. Description of the Client during the Interview

Here, you might want to indicate the client's physical appearance, including height and weight, dress, posture, gestures, facial expressions, voice quality, tensions; how the client seemed to relate to you in the session; client's readiness of response, motivation, warmth, distance, passivity; and so on. Does there appear to be any perceptual or sensory functions that intrude on the interaction? (Document with your observations.) What is the general level of information, vocabulary, judgment, abstraction abilities displayed by the client? What is the stream of thought, regularity, and rate of talking? Are the client's remarks logical? Connected to one another?

VII. Summary and Recommendations

In this section you will want to acknowledge any connections that appear to exist between the client's statement of a problem and other information collected in this session. What is your understanding of the problem? What are the anticipated outcomes of counseling for this person? What type of counselor do you think would best fit this client? If you are to be this client's counselor, which of your characteristics might be particularly helpful? Which might be particularly unhelpful? How realistic are the client's goals for counseling? How long do you think counseling might continue?

    In writing up the intake interview, there are a few cautions to be made. First, avoid psychological jargon. It is not as understandable as you might think! Avoid elaborate inferences. Remember, an inference is a guess—

sometimes an educated guess. An inference can also be wrong. Try to prevent your own biases from entering the report.

USING INTAKE-INTERVIEW INFORMATION

Following the intake interview, but preceding the second session, you will want to review the write-up of the intake interview. Counselors develop different approaches to using this information. Some counselors look primarily for patterns of behavior. For example, one counselor noted that the client had a pattern of incompletions in life; for example, he received a general discharge from the army prior to completing his enlistment, dropped out of college twice, and had a long history of broken relationships. This observation provided food for thought. What happens to this person as he becomes involved in a commitment? What has he come to think of himself as a result of this history? How does he anticipate future commitments?

Another counselor uses the intake information to look for signals that suggest how she might enter the counseling relationship. Is there anything to indicate how the client might relate to females? Is there something in the client's life at present that common sense would suggest is a potential area for counseling attention; for example, is the client in the midst of a divorce? Is the client at a critical developmental stage? The main caution is to avoid reading too much into the intake information. It is far too early for you to begin making interpretations about your client.

OPENING SUBSEQUENT INTERVIEWS

If your first interview was used to collect information about the client, it will be important to focus on developing a therapeutic relationship in subsequent sessions. We refer you to the beginning of this chapter and to Chapter 2 for ways to develop this goal. Once you have established a relationship or rapport with your client, subsequent interviews will require that you reinstate the relationship that has developed. Reinstating the relationship usually amounts to acknowledging the client's absence since the last interview. This includes being sensitive to how your client's world may have changed since your last contact and your reactions in seeing the client again. This can be done with a few short statements, such as, "Hello, _____. It's nice to see you again." This might be followed by some observation about the client's appearance: "You look a little hassled today," or "You're looking more energetic today." Or you might begin by asking, "How are you feeling today?" These types of questions focus on the client's current or immediate condition and reduce the likelihood that the client will spend the major part of the session recounting how the week has gone. If your client needs a bit of small talk to get started, it probably means that he or she needs time to make the transition into the role of help seeker or help taker. The important point is that you probably will not need to go to the same lengths in establishing rapport as was necessary when counseling was first initiated.

TERMINATING THE INTERVIEW

The beginning counselor is often unsure about *when* to terminate, and may feel ready to conclude either before or after the client is ready. A general rule of thumb is to limit the interview to a certain amount of time, such as 45 or 50 minutes. Rarely does a counseling interview need to exceed an hour in length, as both client and counselor have a saturation point.

There is also a minimal amount of time required for counseling to take place. Interviews that continue for no more than 10 or 15 minutes make it very difficult for the counselor to know enough about the client's concern to react appropriately. Indeed, counselors sometimes require 5 to 10 minutes just to reorient themselves and to change their frame of reference from their preceding attention-involving activity to the present activity of counseling.

Acceptance of time limits is especially important when the client has a series of interviews. Research has shown that clients, like everyone else, tend to postpone talking about their concerns as long as possible. Without time limits, the presumed one-hour interview may extend well beyond an hour as a result of this postponing tendency. It is the one instance in which the client can easily manipulate the counselor.

Benjamin has identified two factors basic to the closing process of the interview:

1. *Both the client and the counselor should be aware that the closing is taking place.*
2. *Termination is concerned with what has already taken place; therefore no new material should be introduced or discussed at this phase of the interview. This can be a touchy situation for the counselor when the client suddenly introduces a new topic at the end of the interview. Generally it is best to suggest discussing the new material at the next interview when more time is available: "That sounds like a good place to begin next week." The rare exception to this would be when the client presents an urgent,*

immediate problem that he is really unable to handle.
(1987, p. 29)

Other Termination Strategies

Often a brief and to-the-point statement by the counselor will suffice for closing the interview:

"It looks as if our time is up for today."
"Well, I think it's time to stop for today."

This type of statement may be preceded by a pause or by a concluding kind of remark made by the client.

Another effective way is to use *summarization*. Summarization provides continuity to the interview, is an active kind of counselor response, and often helps the client to hear what he or she has been saying. It is essentially a series of statements in which the counselor ties together the main points of the interview. It should be brief, to the point, and without interpretation. An example of a counselor's using summarization at the end of an interview is the following:

"Essentially, you have indicated that your main concern is with your family—and we have discussed how you might handle your strivings for independence without their interpreting this as rejection."

Another possible termination strategy is to ask the client to summarize or to state how he or she understood what has been going on in the interview, as in the following example:

"As we're ending the session today, I'm wondering what you're taking with you; if you could summarize this, I think it would be helpful to both of us."

Mutual feedback involving both the client and counselor is another possible tool for termination of an interview. If plans and decisions have been made, it is often useful for both the counselor and client to clarify and verify the progress of the interview, as in the following example:

"I guess that's it for today; I'll also be thinking about the decision you're facing. As you understand it, what things do you want to do before our next session?"

▲ EXERCISE 5.2: OPENING AND TERMINATING THE INTERVIEW

Use the following triadic exercise to review styles of opening and terminating the interview. With one of you as the speaker, another as the respondent, and the third as observer, complete the following tasks by using the Observer Rating Charts.

A. Opening the Interview

Speaker: Talk about yourself; share a concern with the listener.

Listener: Respond to the speaker as if you were opening an interview. Try out the responses mentioned in the chapter: unstructured invitation, silence, minimal verbal activity, restatement.

Observer: Observe the kinds of responses made by the listener. Keep a frequency count of the types of responses made. Share your report with the listener.

Recycling: If, as the listener, you did not emit at least two of the four response classes in your interaction with the speaker, complete the interaction again.

Role reversal: Reverse the roles and follow the same process.

B. Terminating the Interview

Speaker: Continue to explore the same topic you introduced in the above interaction.

Listener: Respond to the speaker as if you were terminating an interview. Try out at least one of the procedures mentioned in the section as approaches for termination of the interview (acknowledgment of time limits, summarization, or mutual feedback).

Observer: Observe the procedure for termination used by the listener. Share your report with the listener.

Recycling: If, as the listener, you did not emit any of the termination procedures, or if, for some reason, termination did not occur with your speaker, complete the interaction again.

Role reversal: Reverse the roles and follow the same process.

Record the order and frequency of responses used. If the counselor's first response was an unstructured invitation, place a "1" in the space provided. If the second response was silence, place a "2" in that space. If the third counselor response was a restatement, place a "3" in the appropriate space, and so forth.

Observer Rating Chart: Opening the Interview

Counselor Response	*Order*
Unstructured invitation	
Silence	
Restatement	
Reflection of feeling	
Summarization of feeling	
Request for clarification	
Acknowledgment of nonverbal behavior	

Observer Rating Chart: Terminating the Interview

Counselor Response	*Order*
Time limits	
Summarization of feelings	
Mutual feedback	
Silence	
Structuring next session (time, date, etc.)	

TERMINATING THE COUNSELING RELATIONSHIP

The process of terminating a counseling relationship can evoke various and even conflicting reactions for the counselor. Some may think of it as a loss experience if the relationship has been highly meaningful (Kottler, 1991). Others may consider termination to be an index of the counselor's success. From the client's point of view, termination may be a symbol of success or it may be a "recapitulation of the multiple goodbyes in life" (Hansen, Stevic, & Warner, 1982, p. 306). Whatever the interpretation, it is apparent that termination possesses an emotional dimension that can be intense.

Perhaps the most useful way to conceptualize termination is to think of it as a transition rather than an event (Cormier & Hackney, 1992). As the counseling relationship develops and as the client is able to address and resolve the issues that necessitated counseling, the prospect of termination becomes a therapeutic stage in the process. More often than not, the counselor becomes aware of the approaching termination first. Concerns related to the timing of termination, the preparation for termination, and the anticipation of therapeutic problems related to termination become dominant in the counselor's mind.

When Should Termination Occur?

Some counseling theories provide guidelines for the timing of termination. These include such possibilities as letting the client determine the timing or having the counselor establish the date of termination at the outset of counseling (Cormier & Hackney, 1992). Such issues will be dependent on your own theoretical orientation. However, there are some pragmatic factors that contribute to the question of timing. Cormier and Hackney (1992) have summarized these pragmatic considerations as follows:

1. When counseling has been predicated on a behavioral or other form of contract, progress toward the goals or conditions of the contract presents a clear picture of when counseling should end.
2. When clients feel that their goals have been accomplished, they may initiate termination.
3. When the relationship appears not to be helpful, either to the counselor or client, termination is appropriate.
4. When contextual conditions change—for example, the client or counselor moves to a new location—termination must occur.

Preparing Clients for Termination

Clients should be made aware throughout the process of counseling that there will come a time when counseling is no longer appropriate. This does not mean that they will have worked out all their issues, nor will it mean that they have acquired all the tools and awareness necessary for a happy life. It does mean that they have grown to the point at which they have more to gain from being independent of the counseling relationship than they would gain from continuing the relationship. The authors take this position because we believe that human beings are happier and more self-fulfilled when they are able to trust their own resources. Of course, healthy people rely on others, but they do so out of self-perceived choice rather than self-perceived necessity. As Kottler observed, "Effective therapists are skilled at trying to help their client end in a way, *any* way, that allows them to feel good about their work and continue to be their own therapist in the future" (1991, p. 171).

Occasionally you will know in the first session with your client that the relationship will last a certain length of time. For example, if your client is seeking premarital counseling and the wedding is to take place in two months, the time constraints are apparent. People going to university counseling centers may know that vacations dictate the amount of time allowed for counseling. In such cases, it is appropriate to acknowledge throughout the relationship that these time constraints exist.

When the relationship is more open ended and determined by the client's progress, the termination stage begins well before the final session. The authors believe that for any relationship that has existed more than three months, the topic should be raised three to four weeks prior to termination. This allows the client time to think about and discuss the ramifications of ending counseling with the counselor.

Introducing Termination

Termination need not be presented as a major event. In fact, it is probably better to play it down rather than to play it up. If your clients' reactions suggest that it is a major event for them, then you can respond to that. It is better to acknowledge it as a fact rather than as an experience. This can be done by saying something on the order of:

> "We've been dealing with a lot of issues and I believe you've made a lot of progress. One of our goals all along has been to reach the point where counseling is no longer needed. I think we're reaching that point, and probably in about three or four weeks, we'll be stopping."

You can anticipate that your clients will have any of several reactions to this. They may feel good about their progress, nervous about the prospect of being on their own, or sad to see a significant relationship ending, to name but a few reactions.

Occasionally it is appropriate to terminate gradually. This can be done by spacing the time between interviews. If you have been seeing your client weekly, change the appointments to every other week or once a month. Or you may schedule a six-month check-in that gives your client the sense of an ongoing relationship, one that leaves the door open, should that be necessary. Even with these gradual transitions, you will still have as a major concern the transition of a significant relationship.

In all cases it is important to emphasize the client's continued growth once counseling has ended. This includes summations of what the client has learned in counseling, discussions of other resources and support systems the client can make use of in her or his life, and the invitation for follow up sessions as necessary. Kottler observed that "some people believe that therapy never ceases, that clients continue their dialogues with us (as they do with deceased parents) for the rest of their lives" (1991, p. 173).

Finally, it occasionally happens that the ending of a counseling relationship has a character of finality. Perhaps you or your client is moving. Or you may be referring your client to another help provider. In such instances there may be a grieving process connected with termination. It is appropriate to view this grieving process as necessary and therapeutic in its own right. It is as important for the counselor as for the client. Occasionally a client may terminate simply by canceling the next appointment and there is no formal termination that occurs, yet the helper may still feel some grief. It is a symbolic or ceremonious conclusion, an acknowledgment that the relationship had importance and that reality dictates that it end. In such cases, it is better not to hang on to it; that would only make the transition more difficult. If you are making a referral to another counselor, you must give up your role as helper for both ethical and practical reasons.

SUMMARY

While it is true that the experienced counselor has developed a style for managing the counseling session, beginning counselors must experiment with a variety of behaviors before a style begins to emerge. The verbal interventions included in this chapter are one way to begin defining that style. It is not assumed that all strategies will be comfortable or appropriate to every counselor trainee. Along the way, the beginning counselor is often confronted by misconceptions about helping, about client behavior, and about expectations.

In Chapter 2 we introduced the notion of counselor intentionality as a dimension of the helping relationship. If you will recall, the intentional counselor is one who can function in the interview with alternative behaviors and can conceptualize from different vantage points. These skills are particularly important in the initial interview and in opening subsequent interviews. In some counseling settings, an intake interview will be required. Although the intake procedure is well defined in terms of the type of information to be obtained, the counselor's skills in establishing rapport, soliciting relevant information, and reassuring the client require more than an outline of topics.

The skills of interview termination and case termination call for a counselor who possesses a repertoire of counseling skills and strategies. If termination is viewed as a transition from one psychological condition to another, the counselor functions as the bridge between those two conditions. Developing termination skills that are both natural to your personal style and effective in helping clients to make necessary adjustments will require time and experience. For the moment, it will suffice for you to understand the dynamics of the process and begin to address the matter of skill building.

DISCUSSION QUESTIONS

1. Communication patterns are learned from others, frequently from parents. The rapidity of speech, the use of pauses or junctures, the animation of speech can be attributed more to the influence of significant others than to the commitment of a communicated message. Who do you believe has been most influential in the evolution of your communication patterns?

2. What do you believe are the essential elements of a counseling relationship? As counselor, what are your contributions to the relationship?

3. Discuss what it might be like to be a client seeking help for the first time from an unknown counselor.

4. Discuss the positive perceptions that a client might have after going through an intake interview.

5. What do you think are the most important elements, from a counselor's perspective, in terminating a significant relationship? From the client's perspective?

6. Why is it not ethical to begin or to continue helping a client who is also receiving counseling from another therapist?

RECOMMENDED READINGS

Benjamin, A. *The helping interview* (4th ed.). Boston: Houghton Mifflin, 1987.

> *Benjamin makes some important statements to the beginning counselor about beginning and terminating the interview, and relates his remarks to the counselor's role. You will find Chapter 2, "Stages," very helpful.*

Brammer, L. M., Shostrom, E. L., & Abrego, J. *Therapeutic psychology: Fundamentals of counseling and psychotherapy* (5th ed.). Englewood Cliffs, NJ: Prentice Hall, 1989.

Chapter 7, "Relationship Strategies and Methods," offers an extensive examination of such topics as opening the interview, identifying feelings, acceptance techniques, structuring techniques, listening techniques, leading techniques, and reassurance.

Cormier, L.S., & Hackney, H. *The professional counselor: A process guide to helping.* Boston: Allyn and Bacon, 1992.

Chapter 11, "Termination and Follow-up," examines the connections that affect the decision to terminate, the process of termination, and factors in making a terminating referral. It also provides a case example of termination.

Kottler, J. (1991). *The compleat therapist.* San Francisco: Jossey-Bass.

Kottler touches on a number of issues in the termination process.

▶ 6

Responding to Cognitive Content

The counselor responds to the client in many ways, both verbally and non-verbally. Since your responses will have an impact on clients and the topics they discuss, it is necessary to be aware of the effect your responses will have. One very important effect deals with the changing pattern of the client's verbal behavior. As the verbal interaction and communication begin, topics arise; some topics are developed, some are modified, and some are diverted into new topics. As an active participant in the counseling process, you must be sure that your responses will influence the *direction* of topic development in such ways as choosing from among the topics that are to be discussed and the length of time allotted to the topics. Responding to client content suggests alternatives and conscious choices that you will have to make in the interview. Then, when one choice has been made, the effect of that choice will become the basis for further alternatives. The following example will illustrate the types of choices you, the counselor, will be making. Suppose your client says:

> *Client:* "I've known what this operation would do to my plans for a long time."

Your choices for responding are several. You could (1) paraphrase the client's remarks; (2) accent the word *operation* or the words *your plans*; (3) ask the question, "What will it do?"; (4) say "mm-hmm"; or (5) present an ability-potential type of response such as, "You are able to anticipate the consequences of the operation."

Obviously, these five stimuli will produce different responses from the client. The client may proceed to talk about the operation, about plans, or about how he or she anticipates events. In any case, your response would shape or mold the topic development, and, as a result, influence the future matters the client discusses.

In this chapter we will be working with content choices of a cognitive nature, as opposed to affective or feeling-type choices. In other words, the emphasis now is on your recognition and demonstrated ability to identify and respond to client thoughts or ideas dealing with *events, people,* or *things.*

RECOGNIZING ALTERNATIVES

Each comment of the client presents alternatives to you in terms of content to which you may respond. How you respond to one alternative will shape the next remark of the client. The counselor's task is to identify accurately the kinds of content presented by the client and the alternatives to which you, as the counselor, can respond.

▲ EXERCISE 6.1: IDENTIFYING ALTERNATIVE TOPICS

To give you practice in identifying topic alternatives, read carefully the following client statements. Then identify and list all the different topics in each client response.

1. "They have, but I don't know just exactly how it does work, but you can sign up to take weekend trips in connection with the Air Force. It would be like duty because you have to qualify for it and you can travel all over the U.S."

   _____

   _____

   _____

   _____

2. "And I thought it was great. And I realize that most people have a bad opinion of women in the service but, uh, they shouldn't really, because a woman is going to be what she is, no matter where she is."

   _____

   _____

   _____

   _____

Feedback

The correct answers to the exercises above are as follows:

1. a. I don't know just exactly how it does work.
   b. You can sign up to take weekend trips in connection with the Air Force.
   c. It would be like duty.
   d. You have to qualify for it.
   e. You can travel all over the U.S.
2. a. I thought it was great.
   b. I realize that most people have a bad opinion of women in the service.
   c. They shouldn't really.
   d. A woman is going to be what she is no matter where she is.

RESPONDING TO ALTERNATIVES

The process of selecting alternatives can best be illustrated by excerpts from actual interviews:

> Client: "I like this type of a setup where you can talk directly to people and talk with them. Uh, I don't like big crowds where I don't know anybody and they don't know me."
>
> Counselor: "You'd rather not be in big crowds."

In this example, the client's response contained two basic communications: (1) I like to talk directly to people and (2) I don't like big crowds in which individuals get lost. The counselor chose to respond to the second communication in the client's response. Had the counselor responded by saying, "You prefer situations that permit you to get to know people," the topic focus would have been on getting to know people and the necessary conditions for this. As it was, the response led to a topic focus on the ambiguity of not knowing people. This does not necessarily mean that one response was more appropriate than the other; it is used only to point out the available alternatives.

A study of counseling typescripts suggests that when the counselor has alternative communications to which he or she may respond, the tendency is to respond to the final component of the response. Perhaps this is because of the immediacy of the final part of the response; but if so, that is a poor criterion. It is more logical that the counselor respond to the part of the client's communication that has greatest bearing on the client's concern and is therefore most important.

The counselor may also be tempted to respond to that portion of the client's communication that he or she finds most interesting. In this case the interview tends to center on those topics that the counselor may identify with or be dealing with personally. Again, the counselor must ensure that the choice of alternative topics reflects a decision about the client's needs rather than the counselor's.

TYPES OF DISCRIMINATING STIMULI

There are several types of responses you can use as stimuli to focus on and elicit specific content expressed in the client's communication. The stimuli presented here can be used specifically to respond to the cognitive content of the client's communication; that is, ideas that deal with *events, people,* and *things.*

Although these are not the only possible ones, four stimulus discriminators will be identified here for this purpose: silence, minimal verbal activity, restatements, and open-ended questions. Emphasis will be directed toward the latter two. The use of silence and minimal verbal stimuli has already been noted in previous chapters. Their use as discriminators will be presented here briefly.

Silence

Silence affects the course of topic development as a discriminative stimulus by indicating that the counselor does not want to select or direct the topic at the given time it is used (see Chapter 4). Although the use of silence gives the counselor much less control over the direction topic development takes, it serves to increase the power of other types of responses. Thus, after you have remained silent for several moments, your next verbal response will be more valued by the client and, as a result, will have more influence in shaping the direction of topic development.

Minimal Verbal Activity

Minimal verbal stimuli are those verbalizations and vocalizations that people use when they are listening to someone else. The most common are "mm-hmm," "mmm," "yes," "oh, " and "I see." They are unobtrusive utterances, but have a significant reinforcing value. That is to say, when an utterance such as "mm-hmm" is used consistently following a particular topic or word, the future occurrence of that particular topic or word increases.

Restatements

The restatement is the repetition of all or a selected portion of the client's previous communication, and it neither adds to nor detracts from the basic communication. It confirms for the client that the counselor has heard the communication. Operationally, the restatement may be defined as a simple, compound, complex, or fragmentary sentence that mirrors the client's previous communication. It is dependent in its grammatical structure on the grammatical structure of the client's previous response. The restatement can be used effectively so long as it is interspersed with other types of counselor responses. Otherwise, it can produce a "parrotlike" effect that has an adverse effect on clients.

Some examples of restatements will help you understand this particular discriminative stimulus.

Client:	"I'm hoping to get a good job this summer."
Counselor:	"You're hoping to get a good job." (*Restatement*)
Client:	"It doesn't look like we'll get a vacation this summer."
Counselor:	"No vacation this summer." (*Restatement*)
Client:	"I like people but I sure get tired of them."
Counselor:	"You like people but you also get tired of them." (*Restatement*)

Now, try your hand with a few restatements:

Client: "This has been a really rough year for me."

You: " You've had a rough year. "

Client: "Probably the worst class I have is literature."

You: " Literature is your worst class. "

Discuss your responses with someone.

Open-Ended Questions

Open-ended questions are ones that require more than a minimal one-word answer by the client. They are introduced with *what, where, when,* or *how.* You will find that it is very difficult to ask questions that clearly place the focus on your client. Typically, when you, the counselor, start asking questions, the client will give a minimal answer and then wait for the next question. In other words, the client has not assumed responsibility for the content of the interview. The purpose of the open-ended question is to prevent the client from answering questions with a yes or no response.

Some examples of open-ended questions include the following:

"What do you like about it?"
"What is keeping you from doing it?"
"How do you feel about it?"
"How is it helping you?"
"When do you feel that way?"
"Where does that occur for you?"

Why questions are usually avoided because clients rarely know the answer.

Open-ended questions can easily be overused in an interview. A beginning counselor often tends to bombard initial clients with questions. Extensive use of questions gives a "ping-pong" effect; the counselor asks, the client answers, and so on, thus the counseling resembles little more than an interrogation process.

Decker (1988) observed that counselors who overuse questions may be acting more out of their own needs rather than trying to help the client in the form of structuring, clarifying, or soliciting information. Examples of situations in which questions are used to meet the *counselor's* needs include:

> Voyeurism—*wanting to know certain things about the client to sat-isfy our own curiosity,*
>
> Narcissism—*wanting to make ourselves look good or look like the expert by the kinds of questions we ask,*
>
> Sadism—*bombarding the client with frequent or painful questions so much as to constitute harassment.* (Kottler, 1991, p. 160)

Occasionally, beginning counselors resort to questions simply because they feel more comfortable with this type of lead. This is a good example in which silence may be used in lieu of another question. Ultimately, learning a variety of alternative verbal leads will help to prevent overuse of questions.

It is also important to note that clients may have very different reactions to questions. Some clients may construe counselor questions as a sign of interest on the counselor's part. Other clients may view questions as intrusive and react by withdrawing. As with all verbal responses, counselors need to monitor closely the effects of their verbal leads, particularly questions, on new clients.

Try out a few open-ended questions for yourself.

Client: "It's hard to admit, but I really have wondered whether college is for me."

You: "_____."

Client: "I've gotten to the point where I can't do anything I'm supposed to do."

You: "_____."

Discuss your responses with someone.

▲ EXERCISE 6.2: IDENTIFYING AND RESPONDING TO COGNITIVE CONTENT

A. Identifying Cognitive Content

To give further practice in identifying cognitive content—thoughts or ideas pertaining to events, people, or things—read carefully the following client statements. Then identify and list the different cognitive topics within each client response.

1. "I'm thinking about either going to graduate school or getting a job—whichever would be better experience is what I'll do."

   _____

   _____

   _____

2. "People can say whatever they want about it, but as far as I'm concerned, my place as a woman is in the home and it will not change."

   _____

   _____

   _____

Feedback
The correct answers to the exercises above are as follows:

1. a. I'm thinking about going to graduate school.
    b. I'm also thinking about getting a job.
    c. I'll do whatever provides the best experience.

2. a. People can say whatever they want to about a woman's place.
    b. I think my place as a woman is in the home.
    c. My opinion about this will not change.

B. Responding to Cognitive Content

The following exercise will give you practice in using restatements and open questions. Read each client statement and then respond with the type of response indicated in parentheses:

1. *Client:* "Yes, I think that the best way to learn a language is to actually live with the people and learn it that way. Um, the first year that I was going back to Germany, I didn't learn very much at all."

    You: (Restatement) " Living with the people is the best way to learn a languge ."

2. Client: "I'd like to know the language, but still I can't carry on a conversation because it isn't used that much in my classes."

    You: (Open-ended question) " Why would you like to know the language? "

3. *Client:* "I wanted to go back to school mostly because of the fact that I thought that there would be someone to lead because I just don't know which direction to go sometimes for a few things."

    You: (Restatement) " You want to go to school so someone will lead in a certain direction "

4. Client: "Well, I know you're supposed to study every night, which I don't do, but I'm not the only one who hasn't studied this semester. A lot of other kids have lost interest too."

    You: (Open-ended question) " Why don't you study every night? "

Discuss your responses with someone.

DISCRIMINATION AND SELECTIVE RESPONDING

The emphasis in this chapter has been on the selective responding to some client messages as opposed to others. When the client presents you with a multiple message, you can respond to all the messages or to only part of them. If you respond to only part of the client's messages, that part to which you do not respond may be dropped by the client in future communications, unless it is very important to the client. In this case, the client may attempt to initiate discussion of the topic once again.

The effects of selective responding require you to be very attuned to yourself and your own issues, and ultimately to be comfortable with yourself, your issues, and your feelings. Effective responses to clients demand a sort of consciousness on your part about yourself. For example, if you are personally uncomfortable with issues such as sexuality, abortion, divorce, and so on, you may avoid responding to the mention of these topics by clients, or if the expression of anger scares you, you may avoid responding to anything that might indicate the client is feeling angry. A major way that counselors become and stay conscious of themselves and their impact on clients is through consultation with a supervisor. We discuss this in greater detail in Chapter 11.

▲ EXERCISE 6.3: SELECTIVE RESPONDING

A. Anticipating Client Responses

Using your responses to the client in Part B of the previous exercise, write what you think would be the client's response to what you said. For example, with response 1, if you had said, "When were you in Germany?" the client might have responded, "I was there from 1989 through 1991."

1. Your response: _____

   _____

   Client's next response: _____

   _____

2. Your response: _____

   _____

   Client's next response: _____

   _____

3. Your response: _____

   _____

   Client's next response: _____

   _____

4. Discuss with another person how your stimulus caused the client to respond in one way rather than another. Did your stimulus discriminate between the various topics the client presented?

B. Observed Practice

One of you, designated as the speaker, will share a concern with the listener. As the speaker, make sure your initial statement contains several different ideas to which anyone could respond. For example, "I'm really having trouble in school. There's just so much work I can't keep up with it. I wonder if I can make good enough grades. I also need to keep my job to have enough money to pay for tuition, but I don't know if I'll continue to be able to work and study at the same time."

1. The respondent's task is to select *one* of the ideas or topics and respond to it by using either a *restatement* or an *open question*. After your initial response, allow the speaker to continue, then respond with either *silence* or a *minimal verbal utterance*.
2. The observer's task is to track the way in which the speaker develops the topic and the course of future topics depending on which part of the communication the listener chose to respond to.
3. After completing this in one triad, reverse the roles and complete the same process two more times.
4. At the end of three practices, discuss what you have noticed about how the listener's choice of responses and topics influences the path of the speaker's communication.

SUMMARY

In this chapter, we have shown that the counselor has numerous response choices, and each choice has a corresponding effect on the client's following statement. In this reciprocal arrangement, both the counselor and the client influence the path that counseling will take in the session. Most therapists would acknowledge the importance of the client's choices, which reflect how the client conceptualizes problems and solutions, self and others, success and failure, responsibility and control. However, they do not always acknowledge that the counselor similarly influences the session by choosing to respond to some messages rather than others, by exploring some issues rather than others—in short, by selecting what becomes the focus of the session.

These counselor choices are made in rather commonplace ways, including silence, minimal vocal utterances, restatements of the clients' message, and open-ended questions. The highly experienced counselor makes these choices almost intuitively; the inexperienced counselor must make these choices deliberately. If the inexperienced counselor relies on intuition, the possibility of making bad choices is about equal to the possibility of making good choices. But what is more important, the inexperienced counselor who is unaware of, and thus is not deliberately making choices, is very likely to lack a sense of what is happening in the process of counseling.

This is the principal point of the chapter. Awareness of your effect through active choices allows you, as counselor, to maintain constant awareness of the process and, to some extent, the outcome of the session.

DISCUSSION QUESTIONS

1. What are some of the conditions that might work against you as you try to recognize the different messages in a client statement?

2. How can a counselor shape or influence the topical direction of a session without even being aware that he or she is doing so?

3. Under what counseling conditions might you want to have your clients talking about events, situations, or people, as opposed to feelings?

4. With yourself or a partner, discuss ideas, beliefs, topics, or issues that are uncomfortable for you to talk about. How might this affect the way in which you respond to clients who present these issues and beliefs?

RECOMMENDED READINGS

Benjamin, A. (1987). *The helping interview*. Boston: Houghton Mifflin.

Chapter 5 "The Question," is an excellent summary of the uses and caveats surrounding this counselor verbal response.

Dillard, T., & Reilly, R. (1988). *Systematic interviewing: Communication skills for professional effectiveness*. Columbus: Merrill.

This book contains a host of examples in the use of questions in both different helping settings and with clients of various ages.

Ivey, A. (1988). *Intentional interviewing and counseling* (2nd ed.). Pacific Grove, CA: Brooks/Cole.

Chapter 3, "Questions: Opening Communication," provides a variety of examples of the ways that questions influence the helping process. Chapter 5, "Hearing the Client Accurately," discusses the use of verbal encouragers and paraphrases or restatements.

Ivey, A. E., Ivey, M. B., & Simek-Downing, L. (1987). *Counseling and psychotherapy* (2nd ed.) Englewood Cliffs, NJ: Prentice Hall.

Chapter 2, "Decisional Counseling," provides an overview of the use of selected skills to influence clients in a predicted direction.

Johnson, D. W. (1986). *Reaching out: Interpersonal effectiveness and self actualization* (3rd ed.). Englewood Cliffs, NJ: Prentice Hall.

Chapters 4 and 7 on "Increasing Your Communication Skills" and "Helpful Listening and Responding" discuss sending and receiving messages, discriminating content, and responding to alternatives.

Sklare, G., Portes, P., & Splete, H. (1985). Developing questioning effectiveness in counseling. *Counselor Education and Supervision, 25*(1), 12–20.

The authors present a model for developing effective questioning skills. This article would be helpful to the counselor trainee who needs help either to understand the effect of questioning or to understand how some types of questioning are more effective than others.

▶ 7

Responding to Affective Content

What are some of the ways you communicate how you feel? When you're "down in the dumps," how does your voice sound? When you're angry, what is your face like? Your mouth? Your eyes? Your jaws? When you're afraid, what are some of the expressions you use to communicate this feeling? Human beings have many ways of communicating their internal states. The set jaw often is associated with determination. The glaring eyes speak for anger, even in the small child. The trembling voice, the soft voice, the downcast eyes—all have their meanings.

Clients use all of the verbal and nonverbal modes to tell the counselor their problems. The emotions that accompany the narrative enrich and modify the message. They give the counselor the events of the clients' world *and* the clients' reactions to those events. These cues are not always easy to read. Clenched teeth can mean more than one thing. The trembling voice only suggests the presence of an intense emotion. A part of being a counselor is putting together the pieces or cues of clients' messages in such a way that you can make reasonably good guesses about the underlying emotion.

As indicated earlier, a client's communication presents alternatives. In addition to alternative cognitive topics, you will find that you are faced with choices between cognitive topics and affective topics. This chapter focuses on the affective message, how to recognize it, and how to reinforce its exploration by clients. As Teyber observed, "Conflicted feelings lie at the heart of enduring and pervasive problems. This affective unfolding is a pivotal point in therapy because it brings the therapist and the client to the emotional basis of the client's problems" (1992, p. 89).*

To review briefly, client communications that deal primarily with people, events, or objects may be described as *cognitive* details. Communications that reflect feelings or emotions may be described as *affective* details. Many messages contain both cognitive and affective components. When this occurs, the affective message may not be obvious in the words of the client. Instead, the feelings may be expressed through nonverbal modes, such as vocal pitch, rapidity of speech, body position, and/or gestures.

THE IMPORTANCE OF RESPONDING TO AFFECTIVE CONTENT

Affective content represents feelings or emotions held by clients. Miller, Wackman, Nunnally, and Miller have defined *feelings* as an internal physical response that is a result of one's expectations and experience in any given situation (1988, p. 91). For example, if a client marries and expects to be happy and is, the client will feel happy. If the client expects to feel happy and is not, the client may feel angry or sad. Frequently, feelings are mixed or "both-and"; that is, for a given situation, a client may feel both happiness and sadness, or anger and pain, or anger and relief, and so on. Thus, feelings do not come out of a vacuum but are the result of the "match or mismatch" between one's experience and expectations (Miller et al., 1988, p. 93).

Clients are often either unaware of their feelings or afraid of them. Many people, including those who learn to be helpers, do not want to feel feelings because of the rules those individuals have made about feelings. In fact, a major rule in dysfunctional families is "Don't feel"—sometimes made more specific like "Don't feel angry" or "Don't feel sad." Little boys may hear "Don't feel sad or cry—you'll be a sissy"; little girls may hear "Be nice—be a good girl—don't say anything angry." Often these rules have the effect of masking or interfering with how people truly feel. One of the most important functions in responding to client messages is to give clients permission to feel their feelings, to allow their feelings just to be, rather than stifling, controlling, or holding them back. Persons who, in fact, have held feelings for a long period of time may tend to hold the feeling in a particular musculature of the body, such as tight shoulders or neck, tense lower back, churning gut, and so on (Kelley, 1974).

When clients are given permission to reveal and release feelings, often their energy and well-being are also increased. This occurs because all of

---

* This and all other material from this source are from *Interpersonal Process in Psychotherapy* by E. Teyber. Copyright © 1992 by Brooks/Cole Publishers. Reprinted by permission.

the deep primary feelings have a survival value (Kelley, 1979). For example, anger allows an individual to protect his or her rights and establish personal boundaries or limits (Kelley, 1979). The capacity to recognize and express anger is the basis for healthy assertiveness. As Kelley observed, "The person who cannot become angry, whose anger is deeply repressed, is severely handicapped. . . . These persons' assertions lack conviction and they are often at the mercy of or emotionally dependent on those who are capable of becoming angry" (1979, p. 25). Moreover, the expression of anger is useful in close relationships to "clear the air" and prevent chronic boredom and resentment from building up. Anger and disgust that are expressed and released prompt subsequent expression of love; pain and sadness that are expressed promote later expression of joy and pleasure; and fear that is discharged allows for greater trust (Kelley, 1974).

When a client's communication contains both cognitive and affective components, some therapists recommend the first priority is to acknowledge the affective pattern of the message. Teyber, for one, noted that in all of the indices a therapist has about how to respond to a client, as a general guideline, "the most productive response is to *respond to the feeling that the client is currently experiencing*" (1992, p. 91).

Teyber also noted that another important function of responding to affective content is to help clients *experience* rather than simply talk about feelings. "Little change occurs until clients are able to stop talking about their emotions in an intellectualized or objective manner, and actually experience their conflicted emotions with the therapist" (1992, p. 95). One way to help the client experience their feelings involves modeling or reflecting the feelings, as we discuss later in this chapter. It is also important to do so when the clients are experiencing the full emotional impact of their issues since change is most likely to occur at that time (Teyber, 1992, p. 95).

VERBAL AND NONVERBAL CUES ASSOCIATED WITH EMOTIONS

You may have wondered how you can identify another person's feelings. Although you cannot feel the client's feelings, you can infer what those feelings are and experience very similar feelings. That is to say, you may be able to know what it is like to feel a certain way. How do you do this? You draw from your own emotional experiences and recall that you, too, have experienced pain, anger, and joy, and remember how they felt. You must first recognize the feeling in your client before you can reproduce a similar feeling in yourself.

To do this you may need to become more aware of, and sensitive to, certain verbal and nonverbal cues that are elements of the client's communication. Some of these cues are referred to as *leakage* since they communicate messages the client did not deliberately intend to have communicated (Ekman & Friesen, 1969). Other cues, primarily verbal, are more deliberately intended and are more easily recognized and identified.

In the case of affective leakage, it is important to account for the inferences you draw. For example, when you say, "The client seems happy," that is an inference. If you say, instead, "The client is smiling, and that may mean that he is happy," then you have accounted for your inference.

The total impact of a client's message includes both verbal and nonverbal elements. The verbal impact means that there are certain nouns, adjectives, adverbs, and verbs that express the client's feelings about something or someone. For example:

"I am really *worried* about school."

The verbal element associated with the client's feelings in this example is the word *worried*. These kinds of words can be called *affect* words. They express some feeling that the client possesses. If an adverb such as *really* or *very* precedes the affect word, this indicates an even stronger intensity of emotion.

Nonverbal Cues to Affect

Nonverbal cues can be seen by observing the client's head and facial movement, position of body, quick movements and gestures, and voice quality. Although no single nonverbal cue can be interpreted accurately alone, each does have meaning as part of a larger pattern, or *gestalt*. Thus, there are relationships between nonverbal and verbal aspects of speech. In addition to the relationship between nonverbal and verbal parts of the message, nonverbal cues may also communicate specific information about the relationship of the people involved in the communicative process—in this case the counselor and the client. Nonverbal cues convey information about the *nature* and *intensity* of emotions, sometimes more accurately than verbal cues. The *nature* of the emotion is communicated nonverbally primarily by *head* cues; the *intensity* of an emotion is communicated both by *head* cues and *body* cues (Ekman & Friesen, 1967).

Close observation of the client's body, nonverbal behavior, and facial expressions in particular can offer important information to the counselor about the nature and intensity of blocked feelings as well as feelings that are starting to emerge. For example, one of us recently saw a client who had been coming in weekly for the last few months. On this particular occasion, the counselor noted that shortly after the client sat down, her face became contorted. She then began to describe a situation that had recently occurred involving a loss of an important relationship. The counselor commented on her facial expression—the tightness of it—and inquired about what she might be holding back. She then immediately cried, and upon release of tears, her face softened and relaxed.

▲ EXERCISE 7.1: IDENTIFYING BEHAVIOR

Pick a partner. Interact for about five minutes. Then each of you, in turn, describe your partner, using the phrase:

"I'm observing that you are _____."

Be sure to describe what you *see*, not how you think the other person feels.

TYPES OF AFFECTIVE MESSAGES

Although there are many different kinds of feelings, most feelings that are identified by words fit into one of four areas: affection, anger, fear, or sadness/depression.

☆*Positive Affect*

Feelings of affection reflect positive or good feelings about oneself and others and indicate positive feelings about interpersonal relationships. Many of them can be identified by certain affect words. Affect word cues that communicate the general feeling of well-being, affection, or satisfaction may be subclassified into five general areas:

Enjoyment	Competence	Love	Happiness	Hope
beautiful	able	close	cheerful	luck
enjoy	can	friendly	content	optimism
good	fulfill	love	delighted	try
nice	great	like	excited	guess
pretty	wonderful	need	happy	wish
satisfy	smart	care	laugh(ed)	want
terrific	respect	want	thrill	
tremendous	worth	choose	dig	

Source: T. J. Crowley, *The conditionability of positive and negative self-reference emotional affect statements in a counseling-type interview.* Unpublished doctoral dissertation. Amherst: University of Massachusetts, 1970.

You can continue to add to this list of affect words related to affection. Can you begin to get the feeling for the message implicit in the usage of words such as these? Certain nonverbal cues often occur simultaneously with affection word cues. The most obvious of these cues are facial ones. The corners of the mouth may turn up to produce the hint of a smile. The eyes may widen slightly. "Worry wrinkles" disappear. Often there is an absence of body tension. The arms and hands may be moved in an open-palm gesture of acceptance, or the communicator may reach out and touch the object of the affection message. When the client is describing feelings about an object or event, there may be increased animation of the face and hands.

Anger

Anger represents an obstruction to be relieved or removed in some way. Different kinds of stimuli often elicit anger. One such stimulus is *frustration*. Others are *threat* and *fear*. Conditions such as competition, jealousy, and thwarted aspirations can become threats that elicit angry responses. Anger often represents negative feelings about oneself and/or others. Many times, fear is concealed by an outburst of anger. In such cases the anger becomes a defensive reaction because the person does not feel safe enough to express fear. Anger is also a cover-up for hurt. Beneath strong aggressive outbursts are often deep feelings of vulnerability and pain. Verbal cues that suggest *anger* may be classified into four general categories:

Attack	Grimness	Defensiveness	Quarrelsomeness
argue	dislike	against	angry
attack	hate	protect	fight
compete	nasty	resent	quarrel
criticize	disgust	guard	argue
fight	surly	prepared	take issue
hit	serious		reject
hurt			disagree
offend			

Source: T. J. Crowley, *The conditionability of positive and negative self-reference emotional affect statements in a counseling-type interview.* Unpublished doctoral dissertation. Amherst: University of Massachusetts, 1970.

You can continue to add to this list of affect words that suggest *anger*. Remember that anger covers a broad group of feelings and can be expressed in many ways. With the expression of anger, the body position may become rigid and tense, or it may be characterized by gross changes in body position or movement if the client is expressing direct dislike of the counselor or someone else in the room. (Mehrabian, 1968). Sometimes anger toward another person or the self may be expressed by *hitting,* which consists of fault finding or petty remarks directed at the object of the anger. For example, in counseling a couple with marital problems, one partner may express this sort of anger by continual verbal attacks on the other person or by incessant remarks of dissatisfaction with the partner. Hitting can also be expressed through nonverbal cues such as finger drumming or foot tapping.

Certain vocal qualities are also associated with anger. Many times the voice will become much louder as the person becomes more rigid in what he or she is saying; if the anger is very intense, the person may even shout. In some instances of intense anger, the feeling may be accompanied by tears. Many times the expression of anger will cause vocal pitch to become higher. With some people, however, the vocal pitch actually is lowered, becoming more controlled and measured. This usually means that the person experiencing the anger is attempting to maintain a level of control over his or her feelings.

Fear

Fear represents a person's reaction to some kind of danger to be avoided. Often this reaction is a withdrawal from a painful or stressful situation, from one's self or from other people and relationships. As such, the person experiencing the emotions of fear may also be isolated and sad or depressed. Fear can also be described as a negative set of feelings about something or someone that results in a need to protect one's self. Verbal cues that suggest fear may be classified into four general categories:

Fear	Doubt	Pain	Avoidance
anxious	failure	awful	flee
bothers	flunk	hurts	run from
concerns	undecided	intense	escape
lonely	mediocre	unpleasant	cut out
nervous	moody	uncomfortable	forget
scare	puzzled	aches	
tense	stupid	torn	
upset	unsure		

Source: T. J. Crowley, *The conditionability of positive and negative self-reference emotional affect statements in a counseling-type interview.* Unpublished doctoral dissertation. Amherst: University of Massachusetts, 1970.

You can continue to add to this list of affect words suggesting *fear*. Remember that fear is a broad category of feelings and can be expressed in many ways.

Several facial cues are associated with fear. The mouth may hang wide open as in shock or startlement; the eyes may also dilate. Fear may cause a furrow to appear between the eyebrows. Fear of the counselor or of the topic at hand may be reflected by the client's avoidance of direct eye contact, although the meaning of this varies among cultures.

Body positions and movements are also associated with the expression of fear. At first, the person experiencing fear may appear to be still in body position or may draw back. However, after this initial period, body movement usually become greater as anxiety increases, resulting in jerky and trembling motions. Although parts of the body may shake, often the hands are tightly clasped, as if giving protection. Tension may also be indicated through actions such as leg swinging, foot tapping, or playing with a ring or other piece of jewelry.

Voice qualities are also indicators of the level of anxiety the client is experiencing. As the level of anxiety increases, the breathing rate becomes faster and breathing becomes more shallow. As anxiety and tension increase, the number of speech disturbances increases. This yields a greater number of cues, such as errors, repetitions, stutterings, and omissions of parts of words or sentences (Mahl, 1963). The rate of speech also increases as anxiety mounts, so an anxious person may speak at a faster than usual rate. The intonation of a depressed person or one in the grip of fear is also a departure from the normal intonation. The voice quality may become more subdued with less inflection, so that the voice takes on more of a monotonal quality.

Sadness

Some of the more common conditions expressed by clients are feelings of sadness, loneliness, or depression. These emotions may be a response to a variety of client conditions, including unsatisfying personal relationships, other environmental conditions, physiological imbalances, or even diet. Verbal cues that suggest sadness, loneliness, or depression include the following:

Sadness	Loneliness	Depression
unhappy	alone	depressing
adrift	abandoned	depressed
sorrowful	isolated	disillusioned

Sadness	**Loneliness**	**Depression**
distressed	missing	weary
grieved	missed	listless
heartsick		discouraged
		despondent
		gloomy

Sadness can also be expressed nonverbally. Cormier and Hackney have observed:

> *Only the most preoccupied counselor will fail to notice some of the behavior correlates of sadness. Looking "down in the mouth," "whipped," or "about to cry," are common characteristics of sadness. Other physical cues include a poor posture or slouching in the chair, eyes averted downward and little eye contact with the counselor, talking in a monotone, staring into space, or general lack of awareness or attention to personal qualities or to self-care. (Cormier & Hackney, 1987, p. 118)*

To summarize, the four main affect areas are those of *affection, anger, fear,* and *sadness/depression*. There are identifiable affect words and nonverbal facial cues, body position and movements, and vocal qualities associated with these feelings. Your awareness of these cues can assist you to identify with some accuracy the feeling state of your client and the affective components of his or her communications. Care must be exercised in interpreting these affective cues since there may be disparate meanings across cultures.

▲ EXERCISE 7.2: IDENTIFYING AFFECT CUES

To give you practice in identifying nonverbal and verbal affect cues, complete the following exercises.

A. Identifying Nonverbal Affect Cues

Select a partner. One of you will be the speaker; the other will be the respondent. The speaker should select a feeling from the following list:

Contentment or happiness
Puzzlement or confusion
Anger

Discouragement

Do not tell the respondent which feeling you have selected. Portray the feeling through nonverbal expressions only. The respondent must accurately identify the behaviors you use to communicate the feeling and should infer the feeling you are portraying. After he or she has done so, choose another and repeat the process. When you have portrayed each feeling, reverse roles and repeat the exercise.

B. Linking Body Cues and Emotions

Many emotions are expressed graphically by descriptions about the body. Smith (1985) has provided an excellent list of some of these. We recommend his exercise, which is to enact each of them with your own body and note the feeling and body sensations that accompany each enactment.

He holds his head high.

He has a tight jaw.

He does not hold his head straight.

His head is cocked.

He looks down his nose.

He keeps a stiff upper lip.

He does not look one in the eye.

He is down in the mouth.

He turns away.

He has shifty eyes.

He has a stiff neck.

He sticks his chest out.

His shoulders are stooped.

His arms are outstretched.

He is heavy-handed.

He puts his best foot forward.

He drags his heels.

He puts his finger on it.

He meets one with open arms.

He is tight-fisted.

He waved me away.

He is shady.

His shoulders are square.

He stoops low.

He sits tall.

He sits straight.

He is tied up in a knot.

He is backward.

He is forward.

He leans on people.

He wants to sit on it.

He is weak in the knees.

He puts his foot down.

He is a high stepper.
(pp. 60–61)*

* This and all other quotations from this source are from *The Body in Psychotherapy* by Edward W. L. Smith. Copyright © 1985 by McFarland & Co. Reprinted by permission.

C. Identifying Verbal Affect Cues

The speaker should select a feeling from the following list:

Surprise
Elation or thrill
Anxiety or tension
Sadness or depression
Seriousness or intensity
Irritation or anger

Do not inform the respondent which feeling you have selected. Verbally express the feeling in one or two sentences. Be certain to include the word itself. The respondent should accurately identify the feeling in two ways:

1. Restate the feeling using the same affect word as the speaker.
2. Restate the feeling using a different affect word but one that reflects the same feeling.

For example:

>   *Speaker:* "I feel *good* about being here."
>   *Respondent:* a. "You feel *good?*"
>   b. "You're *glad* to be here."

Choose another feeling and complete the same process. When you have expressed each feeling, reverse roles and repeat the exercise.

D. Identifying Affective Components

Read the following client statements taken from actual interview type-scripts and identify the affective component(s) in each statement by writing first-person sentences and by underlining the affect word of each client's communication. For example:

>   *Client:* "I'm not the type that would like to do research or, uh, things that don't have any contact directly with people. I *like* to be with people, you know—I feel at home and secure with people."

In this statement the affect word *like* is identified and the following affective components are identified by written sentences using the first person:

1. I enjoy being with people.
2. People help me to feel secure.

3. _____ .

If there is more than one affective component within a given client communication, place an asterisk (*) next to the one that you feel has the greatest bearing on the client's concern. In the above example, asterisk either 1 or 2, depending on which has the greater bearing in your opinion.

Client statements:

1. "Well, uh, I'm happy just being in with people and having them know me."
2. "And, and, uh, you know, they always say that you know some people don't like to be called by a number; well I don't either."
3. "In speech I'm, uh, well, in speech I'm not doing good because I'm afraid to talk in front of a bunch of people . . ."
4. "I would love to go back to Germany; I think it's really fabulous."

VERBAL RESPONSES TO AFFECTIVE CONTENTS

It is too simplistic to say that the counselor communicates understanding of client feelings through attitudes such as empathy and positive regard. Although empathy and positive regard are necessary to the counseling relationship, the means for communicating these conditions also must be identified. Two primary reasons why the counselor may not respond to client feelings are (1) the counselor does not know what would be appropriate ways of responding and/or (2) the counselor "blocks" upon recognizing the client's feelings. Knowing how to respond to client feeling with empathy and positive regard takes more than the possession of these attitudes. The counselor must make sure that these attitudes are communicated through words, statements, and timing.

Teyber (1992) has observed how important it is for clients to receive from counselors a more satisfying response to their feelings than they have gotten from other persons in their past. In order to do so, when working with affective content from clients, counselors must be able to provide a safe and supportive atmosphere, often referred to as a *holding environment* (Teyber, 1992). A holding environment simply means that the counselor is able to allow and stay with or "hold" the client's feelings instead of moving away or distancing from the feelings or the client. In doing this, the counselor acts as a container; that is, the counselor's comfort in exploring and allowing the emergence of client feelings provides the support to help the client contain or hold various feelings that are often viewed by the client as unsafe.

This holding environment is usually dramatically different from what either the young client is experiencing or what an adult client experienced while growing up. If the child was sad or hurt, often the parent responded by withdrawing from the child, shaming the child for feeling that way, or denying the client's feeling (Teyber, 1992, p. 105). In all of these parental reactions, the child's feeling was not heard, validated, or "contained"; as a result, the child learned over time to deny or avoid these feelings. Children are developmentally unable to experience and manage feelings on their own without the presence of another person who can be emotionally present for them and receive and even welcome their feelings. If the parent was unable to help the child "hold" feelings in this manner, it will be up to the counselor to do so. Counselors do this by verbal responses that convey understanding of the client's feelings and by nonverbal responses that convey support and compassion. In this way, the counselor allows clients to know that he or she is "not overwhelmed or threatened by their feelings, does not need to move away from them in any way, and is still fully connected to the relationship" (Teyber, 1992, p. 107).

Blocking refers to the counselor's reaction to client feelings in ways that reduce or restrict his or her helpfulness. For example, the counselor may accurately identify the client's feelings of anger but avoid responding to these feelings for several reasons. The counselor might be afraid that the client will leave if the interaction gets too intense. Or the counselor might not trust his or her own judgment and be afraid of turning the client off with an inaccurate response. Or the counselor might fear that acknowledging the feeling would produce a flood of more intense feelings in the client that would be difficult to handle. Or the counselor might have similar feelings that might be aroused. Client feelings related to sex, self-worth, and achievement are also potential blocks.

As mentioned earlier, the primary problem with blocking is that the counselor does not respond to the client's feelings in a more helpful way than the client received in the past. Teyber (1992) has listed a variety of ways in which counselors may block dealing with client affect appropriately:

> *Become anxious and change the topic*
>
> *Fall silent and emotionally withdraw*
>
> *Become directive and tell the client what to do*
>
> *Interpret what the feelings mean and intentionally distance themselves*

Self-disclose or move into their own feelings

Reassure and explain that everything will be all right

Diminish the client by trying to rescue him or her

Become overidentified with the client and insist that the client make some decision or take some action to manage the feeling. (p. 106)

When you find yourself responding in one of these ways, note what is happening to you and how you are feeling. This is another example of useful topics to talk over with your supervisor (see also Chapter 11).

It is possible to identify certain counselor responses that will assist you to discriminate among affective contents and communicate your understanding of the client's feelings at the same time. Two such responses are *reflection of feelings*, and *summarization of feelings*.

Reflection of Feelings

The reflection-of-feelings response is distinctly different from the restatement response, but the two are often confused. As indicated earlier, the restatement is a paraphrase by the counselor of all or a portion of the *cognitive* content in a client's response, whereas the reflection is a paraphrase of the *affective* portion. When the client's response contains both cognitive and affective components, the counselor must differentiate between the two (see Chapter 8) in order to reflect the affective content.

Reflection of feelings accomplishes precisely what its name indicates: a mirroring of the feeling or emotion present in the client's message. This response helps clients to own and express feelings. The value in this is helping clients to recognize their feelings and to accept those feelings rather than fear them. Initially, clients may defend against feelings because they seem dangerous. People who feel sad may do everything in their power to avoid feeling sad or blue. Ultimately, the client needs to learn to trust feelings; it is the experiencing and expressing the sadness rather than the blocking or numbing out of it that is healing (Brammer, Shostrom, & Abrego, 1989).

The reflection-of-feelings response can occur at different levels. At the most obvious level, the counselor may reflect only the surface feeling of the client. At a deeper level, the counselor may reflect an implied feeling with greater intensity than that originally expressed by the client. The more obvious level occurs when the counselor reflects an affect message that is *overtly* present in the client's message by using a *different* affect word but one that captures the same feeling and intensity expressed by the client, as in the following example:

> *Client:*   "I feel really mad that you interrupted me."
> *Counselor:*   "You're very angry about being interrupted."

The second kind of reflection occurs at a deeper level. This one mirrors an affect message that is only *covertly* expressed or implied in the client's message. Consider, for instance, the implied affect message in "I think we have a really neat relationship." The feeling inherent in the words refers to a positive affect message of *like, enjoy, pleased,* and so forth. Thus, a reflection that picks up on the implied feeling in this communication might be among the following:

"Our relationship is important to you."
"Some good things are in it for you."
"You're *pleased* with the relationship."

This reflection that occurs at a deeper level not only mirrors the *covert* feeling but also must at least match the intensity of the client's feeling and perhaps even reflect greater intensity of feeling. Furthermore, the most effective reflection is one that emphasizes what it is the client *anticipates*; in other words, one that acknowledges the *implied admission* of the client's message. Consider this sort of reflection in the following example. Note that the counselor reflects back the covertly implied feeling with a greater intensity of affect and acknowledges the implied admission—that is, what the client would *like* to do or feel.

> *Client:*   "I feel like I have to be so responsible all the time."
> *Counselor:*   "Sometimes you'd feel relieved just to forget all that responsibility—to say 'to hell with it'—and really let go."

Although empathy and understanding of feelings are not themselves a panacea, they do serve some useful functions in the counseling process. For one thing, empathy enhances emotional proximity, creating an atmosphere of closeness and generating warmth. Also, empathy contributes to a sense of self-acceptance. When one person feels really understood by another, there is often a feeling of relief—"Gee, I'm not so confused and/or mixed up after all"—and a sense of acceptance about oneself—"This other person has understood me without condemning the way I think or feel."

When dealing with clients' emotions, beginning counselors often fall into certain traps. One trap deals with the counselor's own sense of security in handling the client's feelings. Many counselors, out of their own insecurity in the situation, will do inappropriate things that do not communicate their understanding of feelings. An example would be probing for further information. Here, rather than reflect the feelings, the counselor asks a question, as in the following example:

> Client: "So, I'm wondering if you could help me find a new major—
>   I suppose if I did find one I'd just bungle things again."
> Counselor: "What was your old major?"

Although probes are often useful and information is often needed by the counselor, the first task should be to *communicate understanding of feelings.* An appropriate reflection-of-feelings response to the preceding example would be, "You feel that it's pretty futile to try again."

Two other common errors made in response to the client's feelings have been identified by Ginott (1965): (1) responding to the event rather than the feelings involved and (2) responding to something general and abstract rather than specific. In the following exchange, the counselor errs by responding to the event:

> Client: "I really felt left out at that party."
> Counselor: "Did you go to the party with someone or by yourself?"

A better response would be to reflect the client's feeling:

> "You might have felt alone there."

In the following exchange, the counselor errs by responding to something general and abstract rather than specific:

> Client: "I just can't seem to make it here at school with the courses."
> Counselor: "They (the courses) can make you work."

It would have been better to respond to the client and not the courses, as in the following example of a reflection of feeling:

> "You seem to feel pretty discouraged with school and all."

Summarization of Feelings

Summarization of feelings is very similar to reflection of feelings in that it is a response that discriminates between different affective components of the client's communication and communicates understanding of the client's feelings by the counselor. The basic difference in the two responses is one of *number,* or quantity. The reflection of feelings responds to only *one* portion of the client's communication, whereas the summarization of feelings is an integration of several affective components of the client's communication. Thus, summarization of feelings is really an extension of reflection of feelings. In this response, the counselor is attending to a broader class of client response and must have the skill to bring together seemingly diverse elements into a meaningful gestalt (Ivey, Ivey, & Simek-Downing, 1987).

Like the reflection of feelings, summarization of feelings involves reflecting the feelings of the client in your own words. Again, this encompasses not just one feeling but a bringing together of several feelings into a significant pattern.

Although there are some instances in which clients present one predominant feeling, there are other instances in which clients have several feelings going on at the same time. Teyber (1992) noted that two common affective constructions with mixed components include anger-sadness-shame and sadness-anger-guilt. In the first sequence, the primary feeling is often anger but it is a negative response to hurt or sadness. Often, the experiencing of the anger and sadness provokes shame. In the second sequence, the predominant feeling is sadness but it is often connected to anger that has been denied because the expression of it produces guilt. These affective sequences are typically acquired in childhood and are a result of both family of origin rules and interactions. The summarization-of-feelings response can identify the various affective states the client describes or experiences. Consider the following examples:

Client:	"I'm so pissed off at my mother and my wife. They're always on my back, telling me what to do, where to go, how to think—planning my whole life for me. It's been this way for years. I wish I could do something different but I just feel hopeless about it. I wish for once I could be a man and stand up to them but I just keep giving in and giving in."
Counselor:	"You seem to be feeling several things in this situation—first, you're obviously *angry* about their behavior. Also, you feel *sad* and perhaps *ashamed* about your powerlessness to effect any change—is that accurate?"
Client:	"I'm really feeling down and out about my job. It's so hard to find the energy to keep going in day after day. I don't really mind the work but over the years the people there have been so nasty that I don't want to be around them. I know if I weren't the nice person that I am I would probably really tell them a thing or two."
Counselor:	"You're feeling *discouraged* about your job. It also sounds like you're feeling pretty *angry* and *fed up* with your co-workers

but, because of your own niceness, you feel a little *guilty* or *reluctant* to express your irritation with them."

Summarization of feelings is often used instead of reflection of feelings when a client's communication contains many different affective elements rather than just one or two. It can also be used effectively when the interview appears to be bogged down. For example, when one topic has been covered repeatedly or when a dead silence occurs during an interview, summarization can increase the interview pace. By tying together various feelings, summarization can identify a central theme. It also provides direction for the interview, and may thus furnish the needed initiative to get the interview going again.

▲ EXERCISE 7.3: ANALYZING RESPONSES TO AFFECTIVE COMPONENTS

A. Responses to Client Statements

For the following counselor-client interactions, please observe the following directions:

1. Read each interaction carefully.
2. For each client statement, identify, by writing sentences, the various affective components of the communication.
3. For each client statements, write your own response to the affective portion(s). Use both a reflection of feelings and a summarization of feelings for each client statement.
4. For each interaction, analyze the written counselor statement according to whether or not it is an appropriate response to the affective components of the client's communication. Then rate each of the written counselor responses on a scale from 1 to 5, with 1 being "completely inappropriate" and 5 being "completely appropriate."
5. Discuss the rationale for your ratings with someone else.

> *Client:*   "I don't mind school too much. I like it, you know, but sometimes I just want to get away and do something different."
> *Counselor:* "School can be boring at times."

$$(\quad 1 \quad 2 \quad 3 \quad 4 \quad 5 \quad)$$

Reflection of feelings: _____

_____

Summarization of feelings: _____

_____

Client:	"Actually I'm not looking for any kind of answer. It would scare me half to death if I got one. (Laughs) Then I would wonder what was wrong with me."
Counselor:	"There's no need to worry about that."

(1 2 3 4 5)

Reflection of feelings: _____

_____

Summarization of feelings: _____

_____

B. Observed Practice

Complete the following exercise with two other people:

1. One of you, designated as the speaker, should share a personal concern with the respondent.
2. The respondent's task is to respond *only* to affective topics using only the two responses covered in the chapter: reflection of feelings and summarization of feelings.
3. The observer will use the Observer Rating Chart (see page 110) to keep track of the number and kinds of responses used by the listener. This feedback should then be given to the listener.
4. After interacting for approximately 10 minutes, reverse the roles.

SUMMARY

The expression and development of affect is naturally assumed to be part of the process of counseling. However, this does not mean that the beginning counselor will be either comfortable with or sensitive to affective messages. Sometimes affect is implicitly expressed in the client's communication. Or there are times when one type of affect masks a different and perhaps more significant affect, such as anger masking fear. When these conditions exist, it is easy to miss the affective message.

In this chapter we have introduced verbal and nonverbal cues that suggest the presence of affect, the nature of affect, and how to respond

Observer Rating Chart

Counselor Response	Type of Counselor Response	
	Reflection of Feelings	*Summarization of Feelings*
1.		
2.		
3.		
4.		
5.		
6.		
7.		
8.		
9.		
10.		
11.		
12.		
13.		
14.		
15.		
16.		
17.		
18.		
19.		
20.		

selectively to affect. The development of these counseling responses is closely related to the client's perception of counselor empathy. In other words, as you become more accomplished at recognizing affect accurately and responding to it, your behavior will be perceived as increasingly empathic. Reflecting and summarizing client feelings are two particularly helpful counseling responses in communicating your understanding to clients. This is not to suggest that you would want to respond to every perceived feeling. In Chapter 8, we shall consider the process of selective responding to affective or cognitive messages and the effect of your choices on the progress of the interview.

DISCUSSION QUESTIONS

1. When a client's message contains both cognitive and affective components, what conditions might lead you to respond to the affective element?

2. Although the reflection of feelings and the summarization of feelings were mentioned specifically as appropriate responses to affect, they are not the only appropriate responses. What other responses might be appropriate? Why would you consider them appropriate?

3. Often clients are less aware of their feelings than of their thoughts. How might you assist clients to become more aware of their feelings by the way you choose to respond?

4. One of the things we discussed in this chapter is the issue of *counselor blocks*—that is, ways in which a counselor may deliberately or inadvertently avoid responding to client affect. Considering the primary emotions of anger, fear, sadness, and happiness, what affect area do you think you would be most likely to block? How does your history contribute to this?

RECOMMENDED READINGS

Brammer, L. M., Shostrom, E. L., & Abrego, P. J. (1989). *Therapeutic psychology: Fundamentals of counseling and psychotherapy* (5th ed.). Englewood Cliffs, NJ: Prentice Hall.

Chapter 7, "Relationship Strategies and Methods," describes a number of considerations in using reflective skills.

Cormier, W. H., & Cormier, L. S. (1991). *Interviewing strategies for helpers* (3rd ed.). Monterey, CA: Brooks/Cole.

Chapter 4, "Nonverbal Behavior," provides the most comprehensive review of client nonverbal behaviors that are encountered in the interview. Included in the chapter is an Inventory of Nonverbal Behavior, which includes an exhaustive listing of kinesic, paralinguistic, proxemic, environmental, and temporal nonverbals. Chapter 5, "Listening Responses," elaborates on the reflection of feeling response.

Knapp, M. L. (1978). *Nonverbal communication in human interaction* (2nd ed.). New York: Holt, Rinehart & Winston.

Knapp introduces Chapter 10, "The Effects of Vocal Cues Which Accompany Spoken Words," with a quotation from Shakespeare's Othello *(Act IV): "I understand a fury in your words but not the words." He proceeds to discuss paralanguage and the meanings behind the meanings of messages. It is highly relevant reading.*

Miller, S., Wackman, D., Nunnally, E., & Miller, P. (1988). *Connecting with self and others.* Littleton, CO: Interpersonal Communication Programs, Inc.

In this impressive book about effective communication, Chapter 5, "The Awareness Wheel," provides some rich and useful information about understanding feelings.

Pistole, M. C. (1989). Attachment: Implications for counselors. *Journal of Counseling and Development, 68,* 190–193.

This author describes a way of working with client affective issues in the area of attachment and provides a case illustration of the use of the counselor as a "container" by accepting and labeling the client's emotional experience.

Smith, E. (1985). *The body in psychotherapy.* Jefferson, NC: McFarland & Co.

Chapter 5, "Communication with the Body," illustrates a number of ways in which affective cues are leaked through body actions.

Teyber, E. (1992). *Interpersonal process in psychotherapy* (2nd ed.). Pacific Grove, CA: Brooks/Cole.

For anyone wishing to know more about the nuts and bolts of working with affective issues, we highly recommend Chapter 5 in this book, "Responding to Conflicted Emotions."

► 8

Differentiating Between Cognitive and Affective Messages

You have seen in Chapters 6 and 7 that there are many ways of responding to any client statement. Since your responses greatly influence the nature of topic development, you will be faced with the decision of which kind of content to respond to and, thus, emphasize. Very often, the client's particular response contains both a cognitive message and an affect message. Typically, in early interviews the affect message is disguised. The disguises may be thin but nonetheless necessary to the clients. It is their way of protecting themselves until they can determine what kinds of things you are willing to listen to. Once you are able to hear the affect message (and this comes with practice), you will have to make some decisions. It is important that you respond to that portion of the client's communication that you think is most significantly related to the client's concerns. The process of choosing between client cognitive and affective topics is called *differentiation.* Whether you choose to respond to the cognitive portion or the affect portion depends largely on what is happening in the interaction at that moment and on what the client needs. In other words, choosing to respond to the cognitive content serves one objective, whereas choosing to respond to the affect content serves another objective.

Some approaches (for instance, the phenomenological) favor almost an exclusive emphasis on affect, whereas others (such as rational-emotive, reality therapy) suggest that the primary emphasis should be on cognitive process. Of course, there are many variables influencing this sort of emphasis.

In working with one client who intellectualizes frequently, the counselor may focus primarily on affect in an effort to get the client to recognize and accept his or her feelings. However, the same counselor, with another client who intellectualizes, may choose to emphasize cognitive elements if the counseling time is too limited for the client to feel comfortable with emotions after his or her primary defense has been removed. There are certainly times when emphasis on the affective takes precedence over the cognitive area and vice versa. Generally, though, during the interview process it is important to respond to both affective and cognitive topics. This is because, for all clients, there are times when feelings govern thought and times when thoughts and their consequences govern or influence feelings. The important point is not which comes first, but which type of counselor intervention is likely to be the most effective.

SETTING THE STAGE FOR AFFECT

In earlier chapters we noted that, at the outset, it is important to get clients to talk. Clients must be able to talk about themselves, identify and express feelings, identify their own behaviors, and relate to the immediate present. Strong feelings of vulnerability on the part of clients may prevent them from doing anything other than responding to their need for defending and protecting themselves. Reduction of these feelings can release energy previously used by clients for preserving their own image and make that energy available for growth and change. It is *only* at this point that clients can talk about themselves and identify and own their feelings and behaviors.

Thus, your initial objective, or first *process goal*, is to reduce the client's initial anxiety. Therefore, your first strategy with every client is an exploratory one; you must determine the effect your behavior has on the client by the client's initial responses to you.

Generally, responding to affect early in the counseling process is the best strategy for reducing client anxiety. This communicates your acceptance and understanding of these feelings to the client. However, with some clients who avoid emotion and intimacy, your response to their affect message may only induce greater anxiety. With this kind of client, you will have to modify the strategy and respond to cognitive topics; find out how the client thinks and what kind of ideas he or she has.

Counselors who always emphasize feelings to the exclusion of cognitive content impose certain limitations on the counseling process. Some of the limitations of responding only to feelings include the following:

1. Responding only to feelings is unrealistic and therefore reduces the possibility of the client's being able to generalize aspects of the

counseling relationship to other relationships. For most clients it is highly unlikely that any of their friends or family would take only their feelings into account.
2. Responding only to feelings fosters an internal focus to the exclusion of the world around the client. Clients may become so preoccupied with themselves that the level of their other relationships deteriorates even more.
3. Responding to affect induces catharsis—the ventilation of pent-up feelings and concerns. For some clients this may be all that is necessary. For other clients this is not a sufficient goal. With catharsis there is a greater possibility of reinforcing "sick talk"; that is, the counselor's responses to feelings may only generate more client negative self-referent statements.

On the other hand, responding primarily to cognitive content presents the following limitations:

1. It may reinforce the intellectualization process; that is, it may encourage the client to continue to abstract and deny feelings that are actually influencing his or her behavior.
2. It may not provide the opportunity that the client needs to share and express feelings in a nonjudgmental setting. The counseling relationship may be the only one in which a client can feel that his or her emotions (and consequently, the self) will not be misunderstood.
3. It may continue to repeat a pattern similar to the rules in the client's family of origin in which "feeling talk" is not allowed, encouraged, or explored.

Again, it must be stressed that the initial strategy in the differentiation process is an *exploratory* one. All clients will respond differently to your emphasis on feelings or on cognitive content. Ways in which you may respond with discrimination to the client and some general effects of responding to affective and cognitive messages merit closer study.

TYPES OF DIFFERENTIATING RESPONSES FOR COGNITIVE AND AFFECTIVE CONTENT

Several counselor responses are useful as discriminators for either cognitive or affective portions of the client's message. There are responses that can place emphasis on one component of the message, to the exclusion of other parts of the client's response. Three particularly useful responses are the accent, the *ability-potential response*, and the *confrontation*.

The Accent

The *accent* is a one- or two-word restatement that emphasizes a very small portion of the client's communication. Its effect is that of a question or a request for clarification or elaboration. For example:

> Client: "I'm having a hard time deciding which college to attend, uh ... I'm not used to making decisions, so it's really perplexing to me."
>
> Counselor: "Perplexing?" (Accents an affect word.)

What other words could the counselor have accented in this client response?

1._____ , which would emphasize: cognitive   affective
2._____ , which would emphasize: cognitive   affective

Model Answers

1. "Hard time?"
2. "To you?"

Choosing "hard time?" would have emphasized the affective portion, but accenting "to you?" would have emphasized the cognitive part of the communication.

The use of the accent places emphasis on a particular thought or feeling. Usually it encourages clients to clarify or expand on their previous statement, since it suggests that the counselor does not fully understand the client. It is used most appropriately to highlight a word that seems vague and abstract. Hence, it elicits specificity from the client.

The accent may be used to respond to either the affect or the cognitive message. The client must have used an emotionally laden word in his or her message in order for the counselor to accent the affect. This is one limitation of the accent. For example:

> Client: "I don't think I will make the grades to stay here."

The counselor has no affect word to accent in this statement. However, the cognitive portion could be accented by saying, "Here?" (Accent). However, if the client said:

> Client: "I'm afraid I won't make the grades to stay here."

Then the counselor could respond with "Afraid?" (Accent). The word *afraid*, which is an affect-type word, can be accented or emphasized, thus inviting the client to elaborate on his or her emotional reaction to the possibility of not doing well enough to stay in school. Try your skill with the accent in the following client statements:

1. *Client:* "Things seem pretty bad now."
   You: "_____." (Emphasizing cognitive or affective?)
2. *Client:* "I don't know what to do about it."
   You: "_____." (Emphasizing cognitive or affective?)

The Ability-Potential Response

The *ability-potential response* is one in which the counselor suggests to clients that they have the ability or potential to engage in a specified form of activity. It can be used either as a response to some cognitive portion or to some feeling expressed in the clients' communication. It not only reinforces the clients' sense of control and management of their own lives and affairs but it also communicates the counselor's faith in the clients' ability to act independently. The ability potential can be used to suggest a course of action that is potentially beneficial to the clients as in the following exchange:

> *Client:* "I don't know where I'm going to get the money to pay that bill."
>
> *You:* "You could work for a semester and earn the money."

In other words, you are suggesting that the client has the ability or the potential to pay the bill, should he or she work for a semester and earn the money. Typically, the ability-potential response begins with "you could" or "you can." Like all of the other types of counselor responses that you have been learning, it can be overused. When that happens, it begins to sound unreal, hollow, and meaningless. It is used effectively as a means of identifying alternatives available to the client. It is misused when, in oversimplification, the counselor attempts to suggest or prescribe something as a panacea. The effect of this is to negate or hide the client's feelings of concern.

Make two ability-potential responses in the following client statements:

> *Client:* "I don't know what he'd do; I'm just hanging in thin air because I don't know how he feels about it."
>
> *You:* "___You could ask him how he feels,_____."

Client: "I think I'd like to teach, but I don't know what the requirements and qualifications are."

You: " You can find out what the
requirements + qualifications.   "

The Confrontation

One of the most useful counselor responses is the confrontation. The word
itself has acquired some excess emotional meanings. The confrontation is
sometimes misconstrued to mean lecturing, judging, or acting in some
punitive or hostile manner. A more accurate notion is to regard the confrontation as a response that enables clients to face what they want or feel
they need to avoid. The avoidance might be a resistance to the client's own
feelings or to another person, including the counselor and counseling relationship. The avoidance is usually expressed as one part of a discrepancy
present in the client's behavior. Thus, the confrontation helps the client to
identify a contradiction, a rationalization or excuse, a misinterpretation, or
some sort of dissonance.

The discrepancy or contradiction is usually one of the following types:

1. A discrepancy between what clients say and how they behave (the
   client who says he is a quiet type but who talks freely in the interview).
2. A contradiction between how clients say they feel and how their behaviors suggest they are feeling (the client who says she is comfortable but
   who continues to fidget).
3. A discrepancy between two verbal messages of the client (the client
   who says he wants to change his behavior but who in the next breath
   places all blame for his behavior on his parents or on others).

Operationally, the confrontation is a compound sentence. The statement
establishes a "you said/but look" condition. In other words, the first part of
the compound sentence is the "you said" portion. It repeats a message of
the client. The second part of the compound sentence presents the contradiction or discrepancy—the "but look" of the client message. For example:

"You say school isn't very satisfying, but your grades are excellent."

"You keep putting that job off, and eventually you're going to be back
in the same trap of being mad at yourself."

The first part, or the "you said" portion, need not be stated by the counselor. Instead, it may be implied if the client's discrepancy is obvious. For
example:

Client: "I just can't talk to people I don't know."
Counselor: "[You say . . . (implied part)] But you don't know me."

Using the confrontation suggests doing just what the word implies and *no more.* The confrontation *describes* client messages, *observes* client behavior, and *presents* evidence. However, the confrontation should *not* contain an accusation, evaluation, or problem solution.

The confrontation serves several important purposes:

1. It assists in the client's achievement of *congruency*—that is, a state in which what the client says and how the client behaves correspond.
2. Its use establishes the counselor as a role model for direct and *open communication.* If the counselor is not afraid to confront these contradictions, perhaps the client can be less afraid of them. As Garfield (1986) noted, it helps the client learn to face a negative situation without catastrophic consequences.
3. It is an action-oriented stimulus. Unlike the reflection stimulus that mirrors the client's *feelings,* the confrontation mirrors the client's *behavior.* It is very useful in initiating action plans and behavior change on the client's part, since it is often the avoidance that maintains the client's problematic behavior.

Patterson (1985) observes that all confrontations run the risk of threatening a client, particularly those that focus on myths the clients have believed about themselves and/or their families. For this reason, the use of confrontation must be judicious and well-timed. Since a confrontation is likely to be better received in the presence of high levels of empathy and positive regard, it is often not used in initial or early interviews. Usually, it is a more effective tool once the safety of the relationship has been well established and the client's anxiety level is lowered (Johnson, 1986). It is also useful to phrase a confrontation in a tentative manner and at a point in the session where there is ample time left to discuss the client's reactions to the confrontation. As with any response, it is important to ensure that the counselor is confronting as a way to help the client grow rather than as an indirect way of venting one's own anger or frustration (Patterson, 1985, p. 78).

Try out the confrontation in these client statements:

Client: "I'd really like to take the course, but the grade contract is really tough."

You: "_____

_____."

Client: "I'm not really angry at my father; he's been doing this to me all my life."

You: "_____

_____."

Discuss your responses with someone.

▲ EXERCISE 8.1: DIFFERENTIATING RESPONSES

A. Responding to Client Statements

In the following client statements, identify the *affective* and *cognitive* components of each; differentiate between the alternatives; then write an appropriate counselor response for each. Limit your responses to accent, ability potential, and confrontation. The type of response to use for each client statement is specified below in parentheses. Tell whether you responded to the affective or cognitive portion. Give your rational for doing so.

Client 1:   "On weekends I could stay here—I could probably get dates, but I don't stay here. I go home, or I go to my friends, ' cause I hate staying, just staying right here."
Counselor: (Accent)

Client 2:   "I don't know how to act when I'm out on a date. I don't know what to do."
Counselor: (Ability potential)

Client 3:   "In speech, uh, I'm not doing good—the other day, uh, my instructor, he says to me, uh, you talk like you—like a whisper, as if you're trying to get away."
Counselor: (Confrontation)

Client 4:   "Most of the time, uh, well, I just like to be alone—but, uh, well, here it is really nice. I like, uh, being here. It helps me feel better."
Counselor: (Accent)

Client 5:   "Well, I'm kind of interested in airport management—but I don't know very much about what that kind of job involves."
Counselor: (Ability potential)

Client 6:   "I mean I really do feel much more comfortable alone—most of the time when I'm with somebody else or, uh, with people, I just feel kind of clammy and nervous, you know."

Counselor: (Confrontation)

B. Observed Practice

Complete the following exercise with two other people:

1. One of you, designated as the speaker, should talk about yourself with the respondent.
2. The respondent's task is to:
   a. Identify cognitive and affective topics present in the speaker's communication.
   b. Choose which topic you'll respond to.
   c. Respond using only the three responses covered in the chapter: accent, ability potential, and confrontation.
3. The observer will use the Observer Rating Chart (see page 122) to keep track of the number and kinds of responses used by the respondent.
4. After approximately 10 minutes of interaction, reverse the roles.

EFFECTS OF RESPONDING TO AFFECTIVE CONTENTS

The importance of responding to client feelings as an anxiety-reduction tool has already been mentioned. Generally speaking, responding to affect diminishes the intensity of feelings. For instance, responding to (accepting) strong feelings of anger expressed by the client will reduce their intensity and assist the client in gaining control of them.

The expression of feelings may be an important goal for some clients. Some people have had so little opportunity to express their feelings openly that to find an acceptant listener provides highly beneficial relief.

Responding to affect with acceptance and understanding can also assist clients to incorporate personal feelings and perceptions into their self-image. In other words, the counselor's acceptance of feelings that have been previously denied and labeled as "bad" by the clients suggests that they may have mislabeled these feelings, and thus themselves.

Finally, responding to affect often is the best way to communicate your warmth and involvement with clients. That is, responding to client feelings establishes a high level of trust between you and your clients. It is precisely this kind of trust that enables clients to own their feelings, behaviors, and commitment to behavior change.

Observer Rating Chart

Counselor Response	Type of Counselor Response		
	Accent	Ability Potential	Confrontation
1.			
2.			
3.			
4.			
5.			
6.			
7.			
8.			
9.			
10.			
11.			
12.			
13.			
14.			
15.			
16.			
17.			
18.			
19.			
20.			

EFFECTS OF RESPONDING TO COGNITIVE CONTENTS

We have already noted that responding to cognitive contents can be an anxiety-reduction tool for clients easily threatened by feelings. Thus, there are times when rapport with clients is established more quickly by discovering how they think before wondering how they feel.

It is also important to realize that behavior incorporates both feelings and thoughts. In order to solve problems and make decisions effectively, clients have to be able to think as well as to feel. Responding to cognitive contents assists clients in developing and expressing those thought processes involved in problem solving and decision making.

Because behavior is governed by thoughts as well as feelings, clients need to examine not only what they feel but how they think. Behavior rigidity is often maintained by the kinds of thought patterns present in the clients' repertoires. These may need to be discussed and explored before any behavior change can occur.

Although exploration of feelings is useful to most clients, it is often not sufficient for goal achievement. Once the counseling goals have been established, action plans must be developed to produce goal attainment. Responding to cognitive content goes one step further than responding to affect in that it focuses directly on behavior change.

Once your exploratory objective has been achieved and you have chosen when to emphasize affective content and when to emphasize cognitive content, it is time to develop and implement strategies for each of these areas. There are some strategies that are more effectively used in working with affective material. Other strategies are best implemented when the focus is on behavior rather than feelings.

SUMMARY

The first seven chapters focused on skills that are basic to the helping relationship. In this chapter, we introduced the process by which the counselor makes discriminations—sometimes subtle discriminations—that affect the outcome of a session. Choosing to respond to the cognitive dimension of a client's problems leads the session in one direction. Choosing, instead, to respond to the affective dimension leads in a quite different direction. Knowing which direction to take is close to the core of the therapeutic experience. In the remaining chapters we shall explore this therapeutic core in greater depth and detail.

DISCUSSION QUESTIONS

1. Every counselor has a natural inclination toward feelings or thoughts. That is, when given an option, the counselor will respond to feelings (or choose to respond to thoughts) without thinking about goals. Which would be your natural inclination? What is it about your life, childhood, current wants, and so on, that leads you to this inclination?

2. What do you think you will have to do in order to overcome your natural inclination? What are the conditions in counseling that would justify your responding to feelings, if your natural inclination was to respond to intellectualizations (or vice versa)?

3. If you were a client, would you prefer a counselor whose natural inclinations were toward feelings or toward rational thinking? What would be the advantages for you if you had the counselor you preferred? What would be the disadvantages to you with such a counselor?

RECOMMENDED READINGS

Benjamin, A. (1987). *The helping interview*. Boston: Houghton Mifflin.

Benjamin discusses a range of responses and leads (Chapter 7) used to facilitate the expression of both cognitive and affective content.

Brammer, L., Shostrom, E., & Abrego, P. (1989). *Therapeutic psychology* (5th ed.). Englewood Cliffs, NJ: Prentice Hall.

These authors describe approaches to both cognitive and affective messages.

Hutchins, D., & Cole, C. (1992). *Helping relationships and strategies* (2nd ed.) Pacific Grove, CA: Brooks/Cole.

These authors provide an excellent discussion of the tool of confrontation (Chapter 9).

Johnson, D. W. (1986). *Reaching out: Interpersonal effectiveness and self-actualization*. Englewood Cliffs, NJ: Prentice Hall.

Chapter 10, "Confrontation and Negotiation," presents a series of steps and exercises to help the reader acquire the necessary skills in using the confrontation response effectively.

▶ 9

Conceptualizing Problems and Setting Goals

It is appropriate now to consider some of the larger issues of counseling—namely, the nature of client problems and the establishment of goals that are realistic antecedents to the solution of those problems. There are philosophical questions that underlie these issues, since there is no one way of conceptualizing human problems. We shall not be able to resolve the philosophical problems for you. It may require the greater part of your career to do that. But we shall present a viewpoint that represents our stand at this time. We find it useful because it focuses not only on our clients but also on the world that they return to after each counseling session—a world in which the problems are real.

THE CLIENT'S WORLD

What brings clients to counseling? The answer to this, more than any other question, will reveal your role as counselor. It is a disarmingly simple question, but not one to be taken lightly. We begin with the response:

1. Clients enter counseling when they experience needs that they, alone, are unable to understand or to meet, or when their particular coping strategies to meet needs no longer work.

That is only the beginning of an answer, however. Three processes have been identified and require further elaboration. These are *to recognize a need, to understand that need,* and *to meet that need.*

First, what does it mean to *need* something? It suggests that something is missing, that there is a hole, an emptiness. This condition reflects a dissatisfaction or incompleteness with the status quo. Something other than the status quo is required in order that the need diminish. Since any movement from the status quo involves *change,* implicit in the meeting of a need is a solution involving change.

This brings us to our second response to the original question:

2. The experience of *needing* is a natural part of the process of living and is the means by which we facilitate and enhance that process.

All human beings share certain basic needs. These include the need for security, nourishment, survival, affiliation, love, and self-esteem. Jourard (1963, pp. 33–38) has conceptualized these needs in a way that is useful for counseling. They include the following:

1. *Survival needs:* All people are concerned with self-preservation and safety. This includes psychological safety as well as physical safety. Although people may not always recognize threats to their psychological safety, they do recognize their responses to those threats—namely, increased anxiety, inaccurate or restricted perceptions of the world, and increasingly inappropriate behavior.

2. *Physical needs:* These include the need for nourishment, freedom from pain, rest, and replenishment of energy. When these needs go unmet or become distorted (overeating, migraine headaches) people's responses may inhibit the satisfaction of still other needs (the migraine sufferer finds it difficult to achieve love and sex needs).

3. *Love and sex needs:* These are the needs to become involved in a close personal way with another human being. People grow in their development of these needs and often recognize their intensity only when they have suddenly experienced the loss of a close personal relationship. When these needs are unmet, people question their potential to love and be loved, to be in an extended relationship, or to be able to give to or take from another person.

4. *Status, success, and self-esteem needs:* These are the needs that motivate people to achieve in the eyes of their peers and to gain respect, confidence, or admiration. When these needs are unmet, people lack self-respect and self-confidence, or overreact with excessive and manufactured self-respect and self-confidence.

5. *Mental-health needs:* When these needs are met, people feel like functional human beings. When they are unmet, people are incongruent, disillusioned, disoriented, and vulnerable to despair.

6. *Freedom needs:* These are the needs to feel autonomous, free to make personal choices, or free not to choose. When these needs go unmet, people feel restricted, undervalued, or unappreciated.

7. *Challenge needs:* These are the needs for activity, future orientation, and opportunity. When they are missing, people are vulnerable to boredom, meaninglessness, or emptiness.

8. *Cognitive-clarity needs:* These needs reflect the drive to resolve the conflicts in values, ideas, and commitments that exist in people's lives.

Perhaps you would add to or take away from this list, according to your view of human beings. The point, however, is that all human beings experience needs as a part of living. To experience a need does not set a person apart as unusual, inadequate, or in some other way lacking. On the other hand, human beings are not always adept at recognizing (comprehending) experienced needs, nor do they necessarily possess the skills required to meet needs once the needs are recognized. To recognize and meet one's needs is not necessarily a natural part of the process of living; it must be learned.

The place where persons learn or do not learn what their needs are and how to get them met is in their family of origin. This is where needs are either affirmed and met or shared and rejected. Teyber noted

> Many enduring psychological problems begin when a basic childhood need is blocked . . . and once the need gets consistently or repetitively blocked, the child in growing up will either block the need in the same way his or her environment blocked it to avoid reexperiencing the need or will to try to rise above the need to have it met indirectly or to partially gratify it by a particular style of coping . . .
>
> The client's unmet childhood need does not dissipate or go away as he grows up. The need may be repressed or defended against, but it continues to seek expression. As a result, clients do not give up trying to have the need met. At the same time, the unmet need remains too anxiety-arousing to be expressed directly. So clients try to rise above the unmet need and indirectly, fulfill it by adopting . . . a particular interpersonal coping style. (1992, pp. 150, 153)

For example, an adult client whose early needs for affection were shamed may block current needs for affection and claim, "I don't need anybody's love. I can make it on my own." Yet at some level the unmet need for affection will still try to seek expression and when it does the client will try to cope with it in a particular way, but usually in an unsatisfying or troublesome way.

Clients also experience needs in terms of current life events and may enter therapy when various life stressors or developmental issues become too hard to handle. For example, an adult woman is coping well with her marriage and her job. But as her aging father unexpectedly develops Alzheimer's disease, her world starts to fall apart and she experiences needs now that were either not there or not apparent to her before this event.

This brings us to our third response to the original question:

3. The act of needing is a passive response that must be reframed into an active state, *wanting*, if the need is to be met.

The act of wanting requires not only that people acknowledge and comprehend the need they experience; it also requires that they conceptualize or fantasize something in the real world that would satisfy the need. It may be more money, a close friend, or a promotion. Until people are able to identify accurately a want, they are unable to mobilize their capabilities to remove the need. This process gives many people difficulty.

Wants are intentions, desires, and wishes for yourself and others. "Wants are attributes to hope for, activities to accomplish, things to acquire, and even a direction to be energized" (Miller, Wackman, Nunnally, & Miller, 1988, p. 97). These authors noted that when a person connects with what is really wanted, energy is focused and a strong force is released (p. 97). They classified wants into these categories:

1. To be: *honest, respected, liked, appreciated, successful, healthy, helpful.*
2. To do: general—*compete, win, collaborate, get even, inquire, clarify, destroy, demand, listen, persuade, understand, undermine, support.* Specific—*finish a project, read the newspaper, cook supper, talk to parents, increase income, change job.*
3. To have: *a good education, a stimulating job, good friends, a happy family, a nice car, money in savings.* (p. 98)

Wants may start as wishes or hopes but ultimately are translated into specific purposes or goals. Recognizing needs, identifying the want that is related to the needs, specifying one or more goals, and developing a plan for obtaining the goals is why clients, often unknowingly, enter counseling.

Thus far we have drawn a picture of the client as a person who is (1) continually experiencing needs, (2) not always understanding or even recognizing some of those needs, and (3) seeking your assistance when unrecognized and unmet needs become the bigger issue of living. Though this may be an adequate description of the person entering counseling, it fails to embrace the total situation of the client. Any description of clients must also include the world in which they live, including significant others, employment or the setting in which they spend the major portion of the day, expectations for self and others, habits and routines, dreams and fantasies of the future, attitudes toward the past, values and the meanings of life, and methods developed for survival (survival of responsibilities, tensions, disappointments, expectations of others, dashed hopes, etc.). You may wish to refer back to our discussion of the initial interview in Chapter 5 for a review of all of these components, as conceptualizing client problems begins in the initial session.

THE ROLE OF THE COUNSELOR

Based on what we have said about the client who is entering counseling, it follows that you would have some fairly clear responsibilities. These responsibilities are above and beyond creating a favorable climate for counseling—even beyond being a good and caring listener. It is your role to hear the unmet needs as clients describe their problems, and to help them hear those needs as well. It is then necessary to help clients translate these needs into wants in order that the working mode can be translated from a passive to an active one. You must listen for those solutions the client has tried that have become part of the problem, and help the client see this. Next, it is your role to help clients formulate goals that will help meet the needs. From these goals, plans of action may be constructed, implemented, and evaluated. Finally, you must help clients recognize that they are making progress. When clients have lived with problems too long, it is difficult to trust any progress.

The counseling process may often be viewed as an unfolding process in which the outer, more obvious problems precede the more subtle, less obvious problems. As an example, consider a client who comes to counseling with an obvious problem: He cannot fall asleep at night. He has a *physical need* to sleep—a want that is "to do" in nature: to go to sleep easily and promptly. After the insomnia problem has been addressed and the goals and strategies have been formulated to help with this, focus is then directed toward those pressures that led to the insomnia in the first place. Often, this may be the result of old wounds or unmet needs that have become recently reactivated. For instance, he recently lost his job as a result of layoffs; he may now feel lacking in self-respect and self-confidence and have *esteem needs* and "to be" wants: wanting to be respected, valued, and appreciated by himself and by others. These may be carry-over needs from childhood that are now being felt again because of a major loss. He may also have "to have" wants: to have another job, to have money to live on, and so on.

As we attempt to conceptualize or understand problem states, it is important that we keep in mind the client responses that can further complicate and add to the problem. These responses may be above and beyond the client's attempt to solve the problem. They include the following:

1. Beliefs the client may already have that contribute to the problem, impede the solution, or become the problem
2. Feelings, the emotional responses to the problem that often exaggerate the problem, impede the comprehension of the problem, or become the problem
3. Behavior, the habits and routines that are inappropriate responses, and perhaps contributors to the problem
4. Interaction patterns, those established ways of reacting to familiar others, including the miscommunication channels, expectations, self-fulfilling prophesies, and so on.

Problem conceptualization does not come quickly. It comes progressively. After your first session with clients, you will begin to have some hunches about them, their world (and how they view it), and their problems (and how they view them). In subsequent sessions these initial hunches will be modified as you understand your clients better and as your clients understand and report their world to you. There will be mistaken hunches along the way. These are to be accepted as part of the process, too. Acknowledge and discard them. The remainder of this chapter is an extension of the conceptualizing process—that is, conceptualizing the client's goals.

PROCESS AND OUTCOME GOALS

The counseling process involves two types of goals: process goals and outcome goals. *Process goals* are related to the establishment of therapeutic conditions necessary for client change. These are general goals, such as establishing rapport, providing a nonthreatening setting, and possessing and communicating accurate empathy and unconditional regard. They can be generalized to all client relationships and can be considered universal goals. Process goals are your primary responsibility; you cannot expect your clients to help you establish and communicate something like unconditional regard.

Unlike process goals, *outcome goals* will be different for each client. They are the goals directly related to your clients' changes, to be made as a result of counseling. As you are able to help your clients understand their concerns, you will want to help them understand how counseling can be used to respond to these concerns. The two of you will begin to formulate tentative outcome goals together. As counseling continues, the original goals may be modified through better understanding of the problems and through the development of new attitudes and behaviors that will eliminate or reduce problems. Goal setting should be viewed as a flexible process, always subject to modification and refinement. Most importantly, outcome goals are *shared* goals, goals that *both you and your clients* agree to work toward achieving.

Outcome goals that are visible or observable are more useful, since they allow you to know when they have been achieved. Not all outcome goals are stated as visible goals, however. For example, consider these two outcome goals:

1. To help your client develop more fully his or her self-actualizing potential
2. To increase the frequency of positive self-statements at home and at work by 50 percent over the next six weeks

Both of these could be considered to be outcome goals. They might even be so closely related as to be the same in terms of outcomes. Your clients may be much more attracted to such goals as developing their self-actualizing potential. You may want to view the development of self-actualizing potential as a composite of many smaller and more specific goals. To state it a little differently, self-actualizing is a hypothetical state that cannot be observed. It can only be inferred through certain visible and audible behaviors. Using this goal, you have no way of knowing the types of activity that your clients will enter into while proceeding toward the goals. As a result, you and your clients will know very little about what they could be doing in the relationship, and you will have no way of assessing progress toward the desired results. Consequently, the first goal listed above is not as satisfactory as the second, in that it does not provide you or your clients with guidelines for change.

When outcome goals are stated precisely, both you and your clients have a better understanding of what is to be accomplished. This better understanding permits you to work more directly with your client's problems or concerns, and reduces tangential efforts. Equally important are the benefits you are able to realize in working with specific behavioral goals. You are able to enlist the cooperation of your clients more directly, since they are more likely to understand what is to be done. In addition, you are in a better position to select viable techniques and strategies when your clients have specific objectives. Finally, both you and your clients are in a better position to recognize progress—a rewarding experience in its own fight.

It is also important to realize that specific observable statements of outcome are required now by almost all counseling agencies that receive both state and federal funding because they are clues to client progress and effectiveness of the counselor's strategies and interventions. There is also some evidence that clients with varying cross-cultural backgrounds respond similarly and positively to the goal-setting process, although more research needs to continue in this area (Taussig, 1987).

▲ EXERCISE 9.1: GOAL SETTING

Tom is a junior in college. He is bright and personable, but a little shy. He came to counseling with the problem of relating to girls. Specifically, he believes that there is some flaw in his personality that "turns girls off." His reasons for thinking this grow out of his experience with dating. He reports that girls go out with him once or twice and then do not accept any more dates. He admits getting discouraged when he calls a girl for a date and she says she already has a commitment. If this happens twice, he never calls the girl again, assuming that she does not want to date him.

Identify a few goals that you think might be appropriate in working with Tom, given that you know very little about him.

_____

_____

_____

_____

_____

_____

Are your goals specific or vague? How would you and Tom know when you had achieved these goals? Are your goals process or outcome goals? If they are process goals, would you need to involve Tom in their establishment? If they are outcome goals, how would achieving them affect Tom's dating problem?

What speculations could you make regarding Tom's solution to the problem? In what ways might his solutions add to the problem?

THREE ELEMENTS OF GOOD OUTCOME GOALS

Perhaps you have noticed from our previous examples that outcome goals are different from process goals in several respects. A well-stated outcome goal includes the following elements: the *behavior* to be changed, the *conditions* under which the change will occur, and the *level* or amount of change. These elements apply to any outcome goal, whether it is to modify eating patterns, reduce negative self-appraisal, or increase assertive requests or refusals.

The second element of an outcome goal indicates the conditions under which the desired change will occur. It is important to weigh carefully the situations or settings in which the client will attempt a new behavior. You would not want to set your client up to fail by identifying settings in which there was little hope for success. The client might agree to modify eating habits at home during the evening, but not to attempt to modify eating habits at the company dinner on Saturday night.

The third element of outcome goals involves the choice of a suitable and realistic level or amount of the new behavior. That is to say, *how much* of the new behavior will the client attempt? Some clients enter diets with the expectation that they will reduce their consumption from 3,000 calories per day to 900 calories per day. A more realistic goal might be to reduce to 1,500 calories. This brings us to another thought about goals. As we modify goals, we come increasingly closer to the ultimate goals of the client. Each time we set a goal, it is a closer approximation of the results. Successive approximations are very important. They allow the client to set more attainable goals, experience success more often, and make what might be dramatic changes in lifestyle.

▲ EXERCISE 9.2: OUTCOME GOALS

In the following exercise, examples of client outcome goals are presented. Determine which of the three elements of an outcome goal—behavior, condition, or level—may be missing. After each example, list the missing parts, using B for behavior, C for condition, and L for level. Feedback will be provided to you at the end of the exercise.

The following example is provided as an illustration: to increase job placement (behavior) of clients with disabilities seen in a rehabilitation agency (condition) by 30 percent in a one-year time period (level).

Identify the missing parts in the following six outcome goals:

1. To decrease temper tantrums C+L
2. To increase exercise to two times a week over a six-week period

3. To decrease the number of nightly arguments at home with your spouse L

4. To decrease tardiness C + L

5. To reduce aggressive behavior with sibling by 50 percent B

6. To make three positive comments about the strengths of each member of your family during a one-week period

Feedback

1. The missing elements are the condition (C) and level (L) of the goal.

2. This goal specifies the behavior and the level; the condition (C) is missing.

3. The level (L) of the goal is missing.

4. This goal specifies the behavior; the condition (C) and level (L) are missing.

5. The behavior (B) is missing; "aggressive behavior" is a label and does not specify what the person would reduce.

6. This is a complete outcome goal! "Making positive comments" is the behavior; "three of them in one week" is the level; "to each family member" is the condition.

TRANSLATING VAGUE CONCERNS INTO SPECIFIC GOALS

Rarely does a client begin by requesting assistance in achieving specific behavior changes. Instead of saying, "I want to be able to talk to teachers without getting nervous," the client is likely to say, "I am shy." In other words, a personal characteristic has been described rather than the ways in which the characteristic is experienced. It then becomes the counselor's job to help the client describe the ways in which the characteristic could be changed.

Taking nonspecific concerns and translating them into specific goal statements is no easy task for the counselor. You must understand the nature of the client's problem and the conditions under which it occurs before the translation can begin. Even then there are difficulties. Egan has suggested the use of certain future-oriented questions to help guide clients in the goal-setting process:

- *What would this problem situation look like if I were managing it better?*
- *What changes in my present lifestyle would make sense?*
- *What would I be doing differently with the people in my life?*

- *What patterns of behavior would be in place that are not currently in place?*
- *What current patterns of behavior would be eliminated?*
- *What would exist that doesn't exist now?*
- *What would be happening that is not happening now?*
- *What would I have that I don't have now?*
- *What decisions would I have made?*
- *What accomplishments would be in place that are not in place now?*
- *What would this opportunity look like if I developed it? (pp. 278–279)*

What can you expect of yourself and your clients in terms of setting specific goals? First, the goals that are set can never be more specific than your understanding and the client's understanding of the problem. This means that at the outset of counseling, goals are likely to be nonspecific and nonbehavioral. *But nonspecific goals are better than no goal at all.*

As you and your client explore the nature of a particular problem, the type of goal(s) appropriate to the problem should become increasingly clear. This clarification will permit both of you to move in the direction of identifying specific behaviors that, if changed, would alter the problem in a positive way. These specific behaviors can then be formulated into goal statements; as you discuss the client's problems in more detail, you can gradually add the circumstances in which to perform the behaviors and how much or how often the target behaviors might be altered.

After you and your client have established the desired outcome goal together, you can identify some action steps that might help the client to achieve the overall goal or target. These action steps can be thought of as *subgoals*. Subgoals consist of a series of smaller or intermediate steps or tasks that help the client perform the desired behaviors gradually. When several subgoals are identified, these are usually arranged in a sequence or hierarchy. The client completes one subgoal successfully before moving on to another one. By gradually completing the activities represented by subgoals in a successful manner, the client's motivation and energy to change may be reinforced and maintained. Successful completion of subgoals also may reduce potential failure experiences by giving the client greater control over the learning process (Bandura, 1969).

▲ EXERCISE 9.3: OUTLINING GOALS

Assume that Brent has come to you for counseling, complaining of insomnia. As you and Brent probe the facets of his concerns, you can consider the specific changes Brent would like to make. Gradually, these changes can be developed into an outline of desired goals. We refer to this as an outline because the major headings (I and II) represent the two overall or primary outcome goals for Brent; the subheadings reflect the subgoals or activities Brent might perform to achieve the overall goal gradually. Remember that goal setting is a flexible process, and that the goals listed in this outline might change as counseling with Brent progresses.

Outcome Goal I: To be able to go to sleep within an hour of going to bed at least four nights of the week at home.
A. To identify in writing all of his prior solutions for trying to go to sleep (counting sheep, daydreaming, eating a snack, etc.).
B. To substitute these "trying to go to sleep" activities with "trying to stay awake" activities.

Outcome Goal II: To double (50% increase) positive feelings and thoughts about himself over the time in which he receives counseling.

Complete the goal outline for this second outcome goal listed above. You might begin by establishing the criteria that Brent would consider important. You might also consider having Brent describe some of the situations in which he feels good about himself. You may also want to explore how he felt about growing up as a young boy. What could Brent do to achieve his short- and long-range directions? From this kind of information and using your own imagination, construct the specific types of subgoals that would help Brent implement this second outcome goal. Continue this process for outcome goals II and III for Brent.

Outcome Goal II: _____

A. _____

_____

B. _____

_____

C. _____

_____

D. _____

_____

Outcome Goal III: *To* acquire another job at approximately the same salary range within the next six months.

A. _____
_____

B. _____
_____

C. _____
_____

D. _____
_____

Notice the process by which outcome goals are established:

1. They begin as overall goals that are directly related to the client's specific or general concerns or descriptions of a set of problems.
2. Specific and observable subgoals are established which, if achieved, permit the realization of the overall goals.

Thus, goal setting moves from general to specific goals; the specific goals are directly related to the general goal, and the general goal is a reflection of the problems presented to the counselor.

CLIENT RESISTANCE TO GOAL SETTING

Occasionally a client may be hesitant about setting goals or reluctant to work toward change. For instance, upon completing a counseling session with her client, a counselor said, "This was the fourth interview, and I still cannot get him to talk about goals." When this happens, the counselor must deal with the question, "What is the client resisting?"

In working with clients who are resistant to goals, it is helpful to realize that such behavior is purposeful. That is, what the client does or avoids doing achieves some desirable result for the client. Consequently, you may find that the client who resists setting goals may be protecting the behavior that is in need of modification because that behavior is doing something desirable. An example is the chronic smoker. While an individual may recognize the negative consequences of smoking, he or she also clings to the habit, believing that it is a helpful way to deal with a tense situation, that it is relaxing, that it increases enjoyment of a good meal, and so forth.

It becomes your task to get clients to identify what they gain from their current behavior. In so doing, you may determine whether that gain or outcome can be achieved in more desirable ways. For example, a young student may throw paper airplanes out the school window in order to receive attention from peers. Gaining attention may be a desirable outcome. It is the method that is the problem. Therefore, you and your client may consider more appropriate means for gaining increased attention, other than throwing airplanes out the school window.

Sometimes clients resist attempts to establish goals because they feel that the counselor (either overtly or subtly) is pushing them in a certain direction. Unless clients can determine some *personal* goals of counseling, the probability of any change is minimal. You can avoid creating client resistance to goals by encouraging active participation by clients in the goal-setting process.

CLIENT PARTICIPATION IN GOAL SETTING

Often, goal setting is construed to mean that you listen to the client, make a mental assessment of the problem, and prescribe a solution or goal. In fact, such a procedure is doomed to failure. The nature of counseling is such that the client must be involved in the establishment of goals. Otherwise, the client's participation is directionless at best and interferes with counseling at worst.

An example will illustrate this idea. A beginning counselor was seeing a client who was overweight, self-conscious about her appearance, reluctant to enter into social relationships with others because of this self-consciousness, and very lonely. Realizing that the problem of being overweight was an important factor, the counselor informed the client that one goal would be for her (the client) to lose one to three pounds per week, under a doctor's supervision. With this, the client became highly defensive and rejected the counselor's goal, saying, "You sound just like my mother."

Goal setting is highly personal. It requires a great deal of effort and commitment on the client's part. Therefore, the client must select goals that are important enough to make sacrifices to achieve. In the preceding example, the client's resistance could have been prevented if the counselor had moved more slowly, permitting the client to identify for herself the significance of her overweight and the importance of potential weight loss. At this point, both the counselor and client could then work together to determine the specific goals and subgoals that, when achieved, might alleviate the client's concerns. As with other aspects of the counseling relationship, goal setting should be an interactive process for which both you and your client assume responsibility.

SUMMARY

In this chapter, we have entered into the therapeutically active portion of the counseling process. In addition to the interactive process that takes place between counselor and client, the counselor begins to establish an internal analytical process in which the client's world is studied. That *study* is both within the client's context and in the larger context of healthy, productive living. Clients will become involved in this study, often quite naturally, as they unfold their experiences, feelings, and thoughts about themselves and others. Interwoven in this process is an emerging awareness of a different or perhaps better set of conditions, which become translated into *goals*. Some of these goals are related to the counseling relationship. Others are more related to the client's world. Through the recognition and establishment of these goals, the counselor begins to understand the direction counseling will take and can begin to help the client reach that same awareness. We will continue this exploration of the higher-order skills of counseling in Chapter 10.

DISCUSSION QUESTIONS

1. Both the client and the counselor bring their worlds into the counseling session. We indicated that goal setting evolves out of an understanding of the client's world. How might the counselor's world affect that process of goal setting? Should the counselor be concerned about this issue? Why?

2. With yourself or with a roleplaying partner, identify a current problem in your life. Consider the list of Egan's 11 questions found in this chapter. How do these questions help you (or your partner) develop goals and future scenarios for this concern?

3. In the beginning of this chapter, we discussed how unmet childhood needs can be reactivated in adult life. As an exercise first for yourself and then with a client, consider completing the following questions posed by Steinem (1992, pp. 104–105). "Write down on [a piece of paper] . . . the things you wish you had received in your childhood and did not." When you have completed this exercise, you have discovered what your needs for yourself are now.

RECOMMENDED READINGS

Cormier, L. S. & Hackney, H. L. (1992). *The professional counselor: A process guide to helping*. Boston: Allyn and Bacon.

The authors provide a discussion of the effect of goal setting on the client and offer a case illustration of goal setting in Chapter 5, "Developing Counseling Goals."

Cormier, W. H., & Cormier, L. S. (1991). *Interviewing strategies for helpers* (3rd ed.). Monterey, CA: Brooks/Cole.

In Chapter 9, "Selecting and Defining Outcome Goals," the authors provide an in-depth examination of the process of developing outcome goals.

Egan, G. (1990). *The skilled helper: A systematic approach to effective helping* (4th ed.). Monterey, CA: Brooks/Cole.

Goal setting is one of the three dimensions of Egan's helping model. The reader will find a discussion of this stage, including how to construct a new scenario, and crafting new agendas in Chapters 11 and 12.

Miller, S., Wackman, D., Nunnally, E., & Miller, P. (1988). *Connecting with self and others.* Littleton, CO: Interpersonal Communication Programs.

Chapter 5, "The Awareness Wheel," describes the process by which needs are translated into wants.

Taussig, I. M. (1987). Comparative responses of Mexican Americans and Anglo-Americans to early goal setting in a public mental health clinic. *Journal of Counseling Psychology, 34,* 214–217.

This article contrasts the responses of Mexican-American and Anglo-American clients to the goal setting process in counseling.

Teyber, E. (1992). *Interpersonal process in psychotherapy.* Pacific Grove, CA: Brooks/Cole.

In Chapter 7, there is an excellent and thorough discussion of the ways in which client needs impact the counseling process.

▶ 10

Using Counseling Strategies and Interventions

In the previous chapter, we mentioned a variety of factors that contribute to the problems that clients bring to counseling, including feelings, beliefs, behaviors, and interactional patterns. Most problems of clients are complex and multidimensional. To deal effectively with such complex issues, counselors need to equip themselves with a variety of strategies and interventions designed to work with all the various ways in which the problem is manifested. Lazarus noted, "Comprehensive treatment at the very least calls for the correction of irrational beliefs, deviant behaviors, unpleasant feelings, intrusive images, stressful relationships, negative sensations, and possible biochemical imbalance. . . . To ignore any of these modalities is to practice a brand of therapy that is incomplete" (1976, pp. 13–14).

In this chapter, we examine a number of helping strategies or interventions. Those that are presented here have been selected because they are used by counselors of varying theoretical orientations and because, when used in conjunction with each other, treat the *whole* person. The strategies we describe are used to help clients (1) work through feelings, (2) work with belief systems and attitudes, (3) work with behaviors, and (4) work with interactional patterns and relationships.

WORKING WITH CLIENT FEELINGS

As we mentioned in Chapter 7, clients will be unable to change unless counselors respond to their feelings in a different way than has happened in the past. In this section, we describe several ways of working with client feelings to provide a more satisfying response to clients than they have received before.

Permission to Feel

Clients need the support and acceptance of the therapist to be able to feel their feelings. You can use *verbal leads* similar to the following to convey your own acceptance of the client's feelings. However, your acceptance must be genuine; otherwise, clients are likely to sense your own discomfort. Examples of leads to convey permission to feel include:

"It's important to feel this now."
"It's OK to feel just what you are feeling now."
"Allow yourself to feel whatever comes up as we talk."
"It's OK for you to feel sad (angry, etc.)."
"You can show me how painful (irritating, etc.) this is."
"I accept your anger (sadness, etc.)."

At another level, you may wish to have clients give themselves permission to feel by suggesting *permission phrases* that they say or repeat after you, such as:

"It's OK for me to feel this way."
"I can accept my own feelings."
"I can face my sadness (anger, etc.)."
"I can show you how I feel."
"It's OK for me to feel sad (angry, etc.) with you."

Eliciting Feelings

Another strategy is to encourage clients to identify feelings, to acknowledge them, and to allow them to come to full expression. This is often and simply accomplished by using verbal leads or open-ended questions that focus on client feelings and help clients elicit different facets of their emotions. The following examples are particularly helpful:

Can you bring that feeling to life for me and help me understand what it is like for you when you are feeling that?

Do you have an image that captures that feeling, or is there a fantasy that goes along with it for you?

Is there a particular place in your body where you experience that feeling?

Is this a familiar or old feeling? When is the first time you can remember having it? Where were you? Who were you with? How did the other person respond to you?

How old do you feel that you are when you experience that feeling? Can you attach an age to it, such as being 7 years old or 13 years old?

Does this feeling have its own sound or movement? Can you make a sound that would let me hear what it's like or a gesture that would help me see it? (Teyber, 1992, p. 94)

Increasing Body Awareness

Clients can also learn to get in touch with their feelings through the use of strategies that encourage greater awareness of what is occurring within one's body. When a person feels tense, it is usually seen or experienced in the contraction of a muscle or group of muscles. Continued tension results in pain such as a headache or numbness, which occurs from nerve pressure accumulated from the tension. Smith has recommended the following invitation to help clients acquire body awareness:

Close your eyes and just relax for a few moments. Breathe comfortably. (Pause) (Repeat the directions to relax and the pauses until the client seems to be involved in the exercise.) Check out your body to see what you find. Note anything in your body which calls attention to itself. Just monitor your body, inch by inch, from the tips of your toes to the top of your head and down to the tips of your fingers. In particular, note any hot spots, cold spots, tight or tense muscles, pains, tingling, or anything happening in your body. Don't try to edit or change anything, just be aware and note what is happening. (Pause for a minute or two.) Take your time. When you are finished, open your eyes. (Wait until client opens her or his eyes.) (1985, p. 107)

Following this, the counselor asks the client to describe whatever he or she noticed.

Clients also can identify and express feelings by being asked to exaggerate a particular body action (Perls, 1973; Smith, 1985). This strategy is useful because people often make bodily movements that suggest an action that reflects a current and present emotion; it is considered a "slip of the body," much in the way a person says something unintended yet meaningful as in a verbal "slip of the tongue." As Smith (1985) noted, by inviting the client to repeat the action in an exaggerated form, the meaning of the body action usually becomes apparent. Smith gave the following illustration:

> *An example of this is the patient who, while talking about her ex-lover, begins slightly swinging her leg which is crossed over the other leg, knee on knee. The therapist asks her to be aware of her leg and she says, "Oh, I'm just nervous today." So the therapist asks her to exaggerate the movement. She swings her leg in a larger arc, with more force, and declares, "I must want to kick him. But I didn't know I was angry today. Oh, I just remembered what he said last week. I am mad at him!" (1985, p. 110)*

By asking the client to exaggerate the body movement, one finds she has both repressed and inhibited a feeling of anger. When a client's movement is directed toward oneself—for instance, if she has been chewing her cheek—the exaggeration of this would also illustrate how she had taken the feeling of anger toward the ex-lover and directed it back toward herself.

Breathing

Another way to help clients get in touch with and express feelings is through work on breathing. According to Lowen (1965), every emotional problem is manifested in some sort of disturbance in breathing. Perls (1969), the founder of gestalt therapy, connected shallow breathing and sighing with depression, yawning with boredom, and restricted breath with anxiety. Smith observed that effective breathing is necessary for vitality; that insufficient breathing leaves the person in a state like "a fire with an inadequate draft" (1985, p. 119). Healthy breathing involves the entire body (p. 120).

There are numerous ways to work with breathing. The first is to note to the client the occasions in which he or she holds a breath or breathes in a shallow or constricted manner. For some clients, it may be useful to teach them the art of deep breathing, in which the breath is started (inhaled) in the abdomen, moves up through the chest, and is released thoroughly in the exhalation, often with the aid of a vocal sound. When clients can breathe deeply and do not hold back or interrupt the breathing cycle, they are more likely to experience what they feel.

Incomplete Sentences

Another possibility to help clients elicit and express feelings is with the use of incomplete sentences. Usually, after some work has been done on breathing, the counselor "feeds" the client with an incomplete sentence stem and the client finishes the sentence with the first thing that comes to mind, continuing to say the same root of that sentence with different completions until there is a point at which the client seems finished. Then another sentence stem is "fed" by the counselor.

Examples of incomplete sentences developed by Branden (1971) to elicit feelings include:

Something I'm feeling is . . .
When I look at you I feel . . .
As you look at me I feel . . .
If I felt mad (or scared or shy or happy, etc.), I . . .
One of the things that I do when I feel mad is . . .
One of the things that might make me feel mad is . . .
One of the ways that feeling mad helps me is . . .
A good thing about feeling mad is . . .
A bad thing about feeling mad is . . .
The rule we had in my family about feeling mad was . . .

WORKING WITH CLIENT BELIEFS AND ATTITUDES

Beliefs and attitudes represent meanings, interpretations, or thoughts a client has about a situation—sometimes referred to as *cognitions.* Beliefs are potent because they affect clients' perceptions about themselves, others, and their lives.

Clients encounter all sorts of difficulty based on their beliefs and attitudes because they may be distorted and based on incomplete information. For instance, clients who are repressed or highly anxious tend to view themselves, others, and the world in a negative way (Beck, 1976; Greenberg & Safran, 1981). A major focus of these interventions is on changing the way the client thinks. In this section of the chapter, we describe two related but somewhat different ways of working with client feelings: the A-B-C-D-E analysis and cognitive restructuring.

A-B-C-D-E Analysis

The A-B-C-D-E analysis is an intervention strategy based on a cognitive counseling approach known as rational-emotive therapy, developed by a psychotherapist named Albert Ellis. According to Ellis, emotional distress is created by faulty, illogical, or irrational thoughts. In other words, if someone feels emotionally upset, it is not a person or a situation that creates the emotional upset but rather the individual's beliefs or thoughts about the situation. Reduction in emotional distress is created when the individual's irrational thinking is changed to rational thinking, through interventions such as the A-B-C-D-E analysis.

In the first part of this strategy, the client learns to recognize the *activating* event (*A*), usually a situation or person that the client finds upsetting. The activating event is often what prompts the client to seek counseling ("My marriage is on the rocks," "I lost my job," "My husband is a jerk," "I don't have any friends," "Why don't boys like me?" "I got passed over for the team," etc.). The most important aspect of this part of the strategy is to refocus clients from attributing their distress to this activating event to their thoughts about it. For example, the counselor might respond, "I realize it is upsetting to you not to make the team; however, it is not this situation in and of itself that is making you feel so bad but rather your thinking about this situation."

In the next part of the strategy, the client's specific thoughts or *beliefs* (*B*) about the activating event are explored and identified. The client may have both rational and irrational thoughts, but it is the irrational thoughts that contribute to the emotional distress and that need to be targeted for change. Rational thoughts are ones that are consistent with reality, are supported by data, and result in *moderate* levels of emotional upset (e.g., "I didn't play as well as other people in the tryouts and they got picked and I didn't"). Irrational thoughts are not based on facts or evidence and lead to high levels of emotional distress (e.g., "Because I didn't make the team I am a jerk"). Irrational beliefs often take the form of either catastrophization ("It will be awful when . . .") or "musturbation" ("I must . . . ," "I should . . . ," "I have to . . . ").

The counselor then links the irrational beliefs with the resulting emotional and behavioral *consequences* (*C*)—that is, what clients feel and how they act as a result (e.g., "I feel so bad, I just can't seem to snap out of it. I didn't want to go back to school because I'm so ashamed of not making the team"). The counselor shows the client how his or her specific irrational beliefs led to these consequences. For instance, the therapist might respond, "You are feeling awful and staying away from school because you now view yourself as a nobody—it is not that you got passed up that is making you feel and act this way, it is the way you're now thinking about yourself."

The real work of the strategy comes next in the *disputation* (*D*) phase. Disputation involves disputing or challenging the client's irrational beliefs with the intent of eliminating them and helping the client acquire more rational thinking. The counselor uses questions to dispute the client's irrational beliefs. Some examples of questions suggested for cognitive disputation by Walen, DiGiuseppe, and Wessler include:

Is that true? Why not?
Can you prove it?
How do you know?
Why is that an overgeneralization?
Why is that a bad term to use?
How would you talk a friend out of such an idea?
What would happen if—?
If that's true, what's the worst that can happen?
So what if that happens?
How would that be so terrible?
Where's the evidence?
How is a disadvantage awful?
Ask yourself, can I still find happiness?
What good things can happen if X occurs?
Can you be happy even if you don't get what you want?
What might happen?
How terrible would that be?
Why would you be done in by that?
What is the probability of a bad consequence?
How will your world be destroyed if X happens?
As long as you believe that, how will you feel?
"Whatever I want, I must get." Where will that get you?
Is it worth it? (1980, pp. 97–99)

When the disputation process has been effective, it will be apparent in new *effects* (E) , such as lessened emotional distress and changes in behavior (e.g., "I still don't like the fact I didn't make the team but I know I am not a jerk just because of that"). It is important for the counselor to help clients recognize when these emotional and behavioral shifts in effects occur.

Cognitive Restructuring

Cognitive or rational restructuring involves not only helping clients learn to recognize and stop self-defeating thoughts but to substitute these thoughts with positive, self-enhancing, or coping thoughts. In the first part of cognitive restructuring, clients learn to stop obsessive, illogical, or negative thoughts as they occur. This involves discrimination training in which they are made aware of what "they tell themselves" before, during, and after problem situations. Clients might be instructed to note and record their negative thoughts before, during, and after stressful or depressing situations for one or two weeks.

After they are aware of the nature and types of their self-defeating thoughts, the counselor helps them work toward identifying more positive or coping thoughts that can replace the negative ones. These coping thoughts are considered to be incompatible with the self-defeating thoughts.

Coping thoughts are designed to help clients picture dealing with problem situations effectively, although not perfectly. In this way, they are considered better than mastery thoughts, which focus on perfection "because they sensitize the clients to possible mistakes and prepare them to recover from errors they may make in real life" (McMullin, 1986, p. 18).* It is best to tailor-make these coping thoughts for each client. Clients also need to learn coping thoughts to use before, during, and after problem situations. For example, a client who fails tests due to anxiety might concentrate on thoughts such as "I will be calm" or "Keep your mind on your studies" before an exam. During an exam, clients learn to concentrate on the exam and to stay calm instead of worrying about flunking or thinking about their nervousness. After using some coping thoughts, clients can be taught to reward or congratulate themselves for coping—instead of punishing themselves for worrying.

When clients have identified some possible alternative coping thoughts to use, they can practice applying these thoughts through overt (roleplay) and covert (imaginary) rehearsal. The rehearsal may take the form of a dialogue or a script and may be read aloud by the client or put on index cards or audiotape. McMullin (1986) observed that for most clients, a period of at least six weeks is necessary for the practice of coping thoughts.

A sample cognitive restructuring dialogue used for rehearsal by an agoraphobic (fear of open spaces) client who feared going to the grocery store alone is provided by McMullin (1986, pp. 19-20).

Coping Dialogue

This morning I'm going to the supermarket. I'll probably be tense in the beginning, but only because I have stayed away from stores for some time—not because stores are really something to fear. Stores are NOT dangerous. Even little children, and very old people go to grocery stores. If stores were dangerous, they'd have a big warning sign in the front which said "WARNING, THE SURGEON GENERAL HAS DETERMINED THAT SUPERMARKETS ARE DANGEROUS TO YOUR HEALTH."

(Client imagines entering store.) "Here I am, looking around! It's just like every other store. There's lots of produce, and canned goods and meats. No one in the history of the world has ever been attacked by a can of peas. Still, I feel a little nervous inside. Since stores don't have the power

---

* This and all other quotations from this source are from *Handbook of Cognitive Therapy Techniques* by R. E. McMullin. Copyright © 1986 by Rian E. McMullin. Reprinted by permission.

to create fear, it must be something I am telling myself. Let's see what superstitious notion I'm buying into. Ah, yes! It's that same old idiotic thought—that I'm going to lose control and embarrass myself in front of all these people. Golden oldie bullshit! I have been saying that nonsense to myself for two years, I have never lost control and I never will. It's just a stupid game I play with myself, like pretending if I put my finger in my ear, my nose will fall off. These people have more things to do in this store than to watch me to see if I show the tiniest sign of tension. They are more interested in finding a ripe tomato. Besides, I don't have to control this tension. All I have to do is buy my can of succotash and leave—big deal! It doesn't matter how tense I get. My job isn't to shop without tension; it's only to shop. And I'm going to shop no matter how I feel. Even if I have to crawl through the checkout line on my hands and knees, I'm going to stay. My life has been ruled by a silly superstition long enough."

(Client completes shopping, leaves store.) "There, I did it! That's the only thing that counts. What I do in life is far more important than how I feel when doing it. I'll keep doing this until I get rid of my superstitions and the fear they produce." (1986, pp. 19–20)

Identifying and internalizing coping thoughts seems to be crucial in order for clients to really benefit from cognitive restructuring. As Meichenbaum asserted, "It appears that the awareness of one's self-statements is a necessary but *not* sufficient condition to cause behavior change. One needs to produce incompatible self-instructions and incompatible behaviors" (1974, p. 51). Gradually, clients should be able to apply their newly found coping skills to the in vivo situations as these occur. If cognitive restructuring is successful, clients can detect increased use of coping thoughts and decreased level of stress in their actual environment. In vivo practice seems crucial for the efficacy of this strategy in order to promote the clients' confidence in their newly learned beliefs.

WORKING WITH CLIENT BEHAVIORS

In the last two decades, there has been an explosion of strategies designed to help clients modify their behavior. Behavioral interventions are based on the assumption that behavior is learned; therefore, inappropriate or maladaptive behavior can be unlearned while more adaptive behavior can be acquired (Wilson, 1989). In this section, we describe three strategies designed to work with client behaviors: social modeling, behavioral rehearsal, and self-management.

Social Modeling

Social modeling, based on observational learning, refers to a process familiar to all human beings. If people are nothing else, they are observers. From earliest childhood, humans watch and imitate. Through this vicarious experience is acquired a great amount of knowledge and skills. The limitations to observational learning include a person's ability to observe, the attractiveness of the model, and the generalizability of the event to be learned.

As a helping strategy, *modeling* is used to help a client acquire desired responses or to extinguish fears—through observing the behavior of another person, the model. This observation can be presented in a live modeling demonstration by the counselor, in symbolic form through written and media-taped models, or through the client's own imagination.

Live Modeling

Live models can include the counselor, who demonstrates the desired behavior, or teachers or peers of the client. Usually you will provide a modeled demonstration by a roleplay activity in which you take the part of the client and show a way to respond or behave. Live modeling is particularly useful in instances in which the client does not have response alternatives available. The modeled demonstration provides cues that the client can use to acquire new responses. For instance, a client who wishes to acquire self-expression skills may benefit from seeing you or a peer demonstrate such skills in roleplayed situations.

Symbolic Modeling

Although live models have much impact on the client, they are often difficult to use because of the lack of control in ensuring their systematic demonstration of the desired behavior. To correct for this, many counselors make use of symbolic models through audiotapes, videotapes, or films in which a desired behavior is introduced and presented. For example, symbolic models could be used with clients who want to improve their study habits. Reading about effective study habits of successful people and their scholastic efforts is a first step to help clients specify those behaviors involved. Next, clients can listen to an audiotape or watch a videotape describing effective study behaviors.

Characteristics of Models

In selecting models, it is best to maximize model-client similarity. Clients are more likely to learn from someone whom they perceive as similar to themselves. Such characteristics as age, sex, prestige, and ethnic background should be considered in selecting effective models. With some clients there is no better model than the client. Hosford and deVisser (1974) have found that arranging conditions so that clients see themselves performing the desired response can be a very powerful learning tool. In their procedure, called *self as a model,* the client's desired behavior is demonstrated to the client on videotape or audiotape. For example, a client who wishes to stop stuttering listens to and practices with a tape in which all stuttering has been edited out. Hosford, Moss, and Morrell (1976) indicated that having a client observe both inappropriate and appropriate behaviors may weaken acquisition of the desired responses and promote occurrence of the undesired behavior.

A coping model may be more helpful than a mastery model (Bornstein & DeVine, 1980). A client may be able to identify more with a model who shows some fear or some struggle in performing than someone who comes across perfectly. For example, a very shy, timid person could be overwhelmed by a very assertive model. This client may improve more quickly if he or she was exposed to a model who starts quietly and gradually increases assertive behaviors. Clients also may learn more from modeling when exposed to more than one model. Multiple models may have more impact on a client, because the client can draw on the strengths and styles of several different persons (Kazdin, 1976).

When modeling fails to contribute to desired client changes, reassess the characteristics of the selected model(s) and the mode and format of the modeled presentation. In many cases, modeling can provide sufficient cues for the client to learn new responses or to extinguish fears. In other instances, modeling may have more effects when accompanied by practices of the target response. Such practices can occur through roleplay and rehearsal strategies, as described in the next section.

Behavior Rehearsal

The strategy of behavior rehearsal uses roleplay and practice attempts to help persons acquire new skills and behave more effectively under threatening or anxiety-producing conditions. Behavior rehearsal is used primarily in three instances:

1. The client does not have and needs to learn the necessary skills to handle a situation (*response acquisition*).
2. The client needs to learn to discriminate between positive and negative application of the skills or between inappropriate and appropriate times and places to use the skills (*response facilitation*).

3. The client's anxiety about the situation needs to be sufficiently reduced so that the client can use skills already learned, even though they are currently inhibited by anxiety *(response disinhibition).*

For example, if a client wants to increase self-disclosive behavior, but does not know what self-disclosure is or has not learned the skills involved in self-disclosing, the client has a deficient repertoire in self-disclosure and needs to acquire certain skills (response acquisition). On the other hand, there are times when the skills already are in the client's repertoire, but the client needs clarification or discrimination training in when and how to employ the skills (response facilitation). Many times people have self-disclosure skills but use the skills inappropriately. A person may self-disclose too much to someone who is disinterested and withhold personal information from a significant other. In another case, the client's anxiety perhaps has inhibited the skills (response disinhibition). In other words, a client may have learned the skills of appropriate self-disclosure but avoids self-disclosing because of anxiety the client feels in certain self-disclosive situations.

The practicalities of behavior rehearsal consist of a series of graduated practice attempts in which the client rehearses the desired behaviors, starting with a situation that is manageable and is not likely to backfire. The rehearsal attempts may be arranged in a hierarchy according to level of difficulty or stress of different situations. Adequate practice of one situation is required before moving on to another scene. The practice of each scene should be very similar to the situations that occur in the client's environment. To simulate these situations realistically, use any necessary props and portray the other person involved with the client as accurately as possible. This portrayal should include acting out the probable response of this person to the client's new or different behavior.

Behavior rehearsal can be overt or covert. In covert behavior rehearsal, clients practice the target behavior by *imagining* themselves performing the response in certain situations. For instance, clients might imagine themselves successfully presenting an important speech or initiating a discussion with a friend or a boss. In overt rehearsal, the client *acts out* the target responses in roleplayed *scenarios.* Both covert and overt rehearsal seem to be quite effective (Kazdin, 1982). Probably a client could benefit from engaging in both of these forms of behavioral rehearsal. Initially, the client might practice covertly and later act out the responses in roleplayed enactments. Covert rehearsal also can be used easily by clients as homework, since imaginary practice does not require the presence of another person.

Each scene should be practiced before moving on to the next scene. You can determine when a scene is rehearsed satisfactorily by three criteria proposed by Lazarus:

1. *The client is able to enact the scene without feeling anxious.*
2. *The client's general demeanor supports the client's words.*
3. *The client's words and actions would seem fair and reasonable to an objective onlooker (1966, p. 210).*

However, the rehearsal efforts may be limited unless accompanied by some form of feedback or analysis of performance.

Feedback is an important part of roleplay and rehearsal strategies. Feedback is a way for the client to recognize both the problems and successes encountered in the practice attempts. According to Melnick (1973), feedback is a means of observing and evaluating one's performance and of initiating corrective action. However, feedback should not be used indiscriminately. Feedback may be more effective if the client is willing to change, if the feedback given is adequate but not overwhelming, and if the feedback helps the client identify other alternatives (McKeachie, 1976).

Following rehearsal attempts, clients can be encouraged to evaluate their performances. You will be another important source of feedback. Remember to reinforce the client for gradual improvement. Feedback also can be supplied by videotaped and audiotaped playbacks of the client's practices. These taped playbacks may be more objective assessments of the client's performance. At first you can go over the tapes together and point out the strengths and limitations apparent in the practice. Gradually, the client should be able to analyze the taped playback alone—providing self-analysis and self-reinforcement for the practice efforts.

Modeling, Rehearsal, and Feedback: Components of Skill Training

It should be recognized that the strategies of modeling, rehearsal, and feedback can be combined as a skill-training package. These strategies often are used to teach clients problem-solving skills, decision-making skills, communication skills, and assertion skills. For example, in assertion training, you begin by having the client identify one situation in which he or she wants to be more assertive. Then specify what assertive behaviors are involved and what the client would like to say or do. The situation is modeled and roleplayed consistently in the interview until the client can be assertive without experiencing any anxiety. Following successful completion of the task outside the interview, assertion training can continue for other kinds of situations involving self-assertion by the client. Successes at assertiveness will soon generalize to other situations as well; that is, it will become increasingly easier for clients to be assertive on their own without assistance and feedback.

As an illustration, suppose you are working with a student who reports a lack of assertive classroom behaviors. You and your client would first specify the desired assertive skills. The skills selected would be appropriate for the student's age, gender, and cultural background. You may need to observe the student in the classroom setting to identify these target behaviors. In counting the number of times the student engages in assertive classroom behavior (asking questions, voicing opinions, engaging in group discussion, giving reports, volunteering for blackboard work, initiating conversations with the teacher, etc.), you can obtain an accurate idea of the kind of assertive behaviors that are most prevalent in the client's repertoire and the ones the student needs most to strengthen. You can provide either live, symbolic, or covert models of these specific assertive behaviors. After the client has seen, listened to, read about, or imagined these modeled behaviors, the client can demonstrate and practice small steps of such assertive classroom behaviors in the interview. Following practice attempts in which the client is able to demonstrate repeated efforts of a given behavior within the interview, he or she should be encouraged to practice it on a daily basis in the classroom.

Self-Management

Many persons are legitimately concerned about the long-term effects of helping. In an effort to promote enduring client changes, counselors have become more concerned with client self-directed change. This interest has led many counseling researchers and practitioners to explore the usefulness of a variety of helping strategies called *self-control* (Cautela, 1969), or *self-management* (Karoly & Kanfer, 1982).

The primary characteristic of a self-management strategy is that the client administers the strategy and directs the change efforts with minimal assistance from the counselor. Self-management strategies are very useful in dealing with a number of client problems and may promote generalization to life settings of what clients learn in the interview. Self-management strategies are among the best strategies designed to strengthen client investment in the helping process. Self-management may eliminate the counselor as a "middle" person and ensure greater chances of client success because of the investment made by the client in the strategies for change. Two of the most useful self-management strategies include self-monitoring and self-reward.

Self-Monitoring

Recent emphases in behavioral approaches suggest the efficacy of a number of self-control procedures, of which self-monitoring is the primary one. Self-monitoring involves having clients count and/or regulate given habits, thoughts, or feelings. Self-monitoring seems to interfere with the learned habit by breaking the stimulus-response association and by encouraging performance of the desired response—which is then often reinforced by the individual's sense of progress following its accomplishment.

There are two issues that affect the self-monitoring strategy—reactivity and reliability. *Reactivity* means that the process of noticing one's own behavior closely can cause the behavior to change. *Reliability* refers to the accuracy with which the client counts the behavior. For therapy purposes, you and your client should attempt to structure the self-monitoring in a way that maximizes the reactivity. Therefore, in implementing the procedure, you will need to consider what, how, and when to self-monitor.

What to Monitor. An initial step involves selection of the behavior to monitor. Usually individuals will achieve better results with self-monitoring if they start by counting only one behavior—at least initially. Clients may, for example, count positive feelings about themselves or thoughts of competency. The counting encourages greater frequency of these kinds of thoughts and feelings. Clients may count the number of times they tell themselves to do well on a task, or they may count the number of behaviors related to goal achievement (e.g., the number of times they tell their spouse "I love you," the number of times they initiate conversations or participate in class discussions, and so forth). The important thing is that they monitor behaviors that they value and care to change.

How to Monitor. The particular method the client uses to count the target response will depend on the nature of the selected response. Generally, clients will count either the *frequency* or *duration* of a response. If they are interested in knowing how often the response occurs, they can use a frequency count to note the number of times they smoke, talk on the telephone, initiate social conversations, or think about themselves positively. Sometimes it is more useful to know the amount of time the behavior occurs. A person can count the duration or length of a behavior in these cases. For example, clients might count how long they studied, how long they talked on the telephone, or the length of depressed periods of thought. Occasionally, clients may find it useful to record both the frequency and duration of a response. In choosing to count the occurrences of a behavior either by the number or by the amount of time, there is a simple rule of thumb recommended by Watson and Tharp: "If it is easy to count the number of separate times you perform the target behavior, count that. If it is not easy, or if the target behavior runs on for several minutes at a time, count the amount of time you do it" (1972, p. 82).

In some cases where the target response occurs very often or almost continuously, or when the onset and termination of the target responses are hard to detect, the frequency and duration methods of recording may not be too useful. In these instances, clients could record with an interval method. In the interval method of recording, they could divide the time for recording (8:00 A.M. to 8:00 P.M.) into time intervals such as 30 minutes, one hour, or two hours. During each time interval, they simply record the presence or absence of the behavior with a "yes" if the behavior occurred or a "no" if it did not. Ciminero, Nelson, and Lipinski (1977) suggested the information gleaned by the all-or-none interval recording method may be increased if clients are instructed to rate each interval using a number system to indicate how often the target response occurred. For example, using a five-point scale, persons could rate the occurrence of a response as a 0, 1, 2, 3, or 4 depending on whether the response occurred never, occasionally, often, very frequently, or always.

Clients will need to record with the assistance of some device for recording. These can range from simple devices such as notecards, logs, and diaries for written recordings, to more mechanical devices such as a golf wrist counter, a kitchen timer, a wristwatch, or a tape recorder. The device may increase the reactivity of self-monitoring if it is obtrusive; yet it should not be so noticeable that it is embarrassing or awkward for clients to use (Nelson, Lipinski, & Boykin, 1978). The device should be simple to use, convenient, portable, and economical.

When to Record.   The timing of self-monitoring can influence the change produced by this strategy. Generally, there are two times when clients can record: before the response (prebehavior monitoring) or after the response (postbehavior monitoring) (Bellack, Rozensky, & Schwartz, 1974). In prebehavior monitoring, the client reveals the intention or urge to engage in the behavior before doing so. For instance, the client records times when she or he has an urge to eat a dessert or a snack but does not. In postbehavior monitoring, the client records after the behavior has occurred. For example, the client records after each time she or he exercises. The effects of self-monitoring may depend on the timing and on whether there are other factors competing for the client's attention at the time the response is recorded (Nelson, 1977). Although Kanfer (1980) has stated that there are insufficient data to judge whether pre- or postmonitoring is most effective, we suggest the following two rules of thumb:

1. *To decrease the monitored behavior:* Since you want to decrease the number of cigarettes you smoke (or the number of self-critical thoughts you have), each time you have the urge to smoke but do not (or start to criticize yourself but refrain from doing so), then count this on your log.
2. *To increase a behavior:* Since you want to increase the number of times you verbally express your opinions to someone else (or the number of positive, self-enhancing thoughts), count and record on your log immediately after you express an opinion (or as soon as you are aware of thinking something positive about yourself or your accomplishments).

Counting, or quantifying, behaviors is the initial step in self-monitoring. The second and equally important step in self-monitoring is charting or plotting the behavior counts over a period of time. This permits clients to see progress that might not otherwise be apparent. It also permits clients to set daily goals that are more attainable than the overall goal. Clients can take weekly cumulative counts of self-monitored behaviors and chart them on a simple line graph. After graphing the data, the public display of the graph may set the occasion for both self- and external reinforcement.

To summarize, self-monitoring is most likely to produce desired behavioral changes when the following conditions exist:

1. The client is motivated to change the behavior to be monitored.
2. The client monitors a limited number of behaviors and these behaviors are discrete.
3. The monitoring act is closely related in time prior to or after the monitored behavior.
4. The client receives some feedback from the monitoring that is compared with the client's goals (McFall, 1977).

Self-Reward

Research suggests that the effects produced by self-monitoring may be greater and more permanent if self-monitoring is accompanied by other therapeutic strategies, such as self-reward (Mahoney, Moura, & Wade, 1973). Self-monitoring can always be combined with other helping strategies as a way to collect data concerning the occurrence of goal behaviors. As we noted in the previous section, self-monitoring also can be used intentionally to induce therapeutic change. However, the therapeutic gains from self-monitoring may be maximized with the explicit use of other self-management strategies to increase or decrease a response.

Self-reward involves the self-presentation of rewards following the occurrence of a desired behavior. Self-reward is intended to strengthen a behavior. It is assumed that self-reward functions like external reinforcement. A *reinforcer* is something that, when administered following a target response, tends to maintain or increase the probability of that response in the future.

There are two ways clients can use self-reward. First, they can give themselves rewards after engaging in specified behaviors. For example, clients could imagine being on a sailboat after doing daily exercises or could buy themselves treats after daily studying. Or they could remove something negative after performing the desired behaviors. For instance, an overweight client could remove a "fat picture" from the wall after losing a certain number of pounds. In most cases we recommend the first approach (self-presentation of a positive stimulus) because it is more positive than the second. The first approach, which may be referred to as *positive self-reward* has been validated by more research studies than the negative procedure (Mahoney, Moura, & Wade, 1973).

There are three major factors involved in helping a client use a self-reward strategy: what to use as rewards, how to administer the rewards, and when to administer the rewards.

Types of Rewards. First, you will want to help your clients select appropriate rewards. Clients should choose things that are truly reinforcing. There are different types of rewards to use. An example of a verbal-symbolic reward is self-praise, such as thinking, "I really did that well." Imaginal rewards involve visualizing or fantasizing scenes that produce pleasure and satisfaction. Material rewards include tangible events such as an enjoyable activity, a purchase, or tokens or points that can be exchanged for something. Rewards also can be current or potential. A current reward is something enjoyable that occurs on a daily basis, such as eating, reading, or getting the mail. A potential reward is something that could occur in the future that would be satisfying and enjoyable. Taking a trip and going out for a gourmet meal are examples of potential rewards.

Clients should be encouraged to select a variety of rewards, including both current and potential, material, imaginal, and verbal-symbolic. This may prevent one reward from losing its potency or impact. You can help clients select rewards by having them identify some ongoing and potentially satisfying thoughts and activities. An occasional client may have difficulty in identifying rewards. In lieu of using a very enjoyable activity as a reward, this client might choose a more mundane daily activity, such as answering the telephone or walking up or down stairs.

Using a frequently occurring activity as a reward is based on the *Premack principle*, which states that a high-probability behavior can be used to reinforce a low-probability behavior (Premack, 1965). For instance, something a student engages in frequently, such as getting up from the desk, can be made contingent on something the student does infrequently, such as completing assignments or work problems. The rewards used can be tailored to each client, since not all events or fantasies are reinforcing for all persons. The selected rewards should relate to the client's personal history, be acceptable to the client, and be something the client wants to do and is capable of doing (Kanfer, 1980).

Delivery of Rewards. After selecting rewards, clients will need to work out ways to administer the rewards. They should know what has to be done in order to present themselves with a reward. You might encourage them to reward themselves for *gradual* progress toward the desired goal. Daily rewards for small steps are more effective than one delayed reward for a great improvement.

Timing of Rewards. Clients also need to present the rewards at certain times in order to maximize the self-reward strategy. The reward should come only *after* target behavior has been performed in order to have the most impact.

Client Commitment to Self-Management

A critical problem in the effective use of any self-management strategy is having the client use the strategy regularly and consistently. There is some evidence that people who benefit from self-management use self-management strategies on a very consistent basis (Perri & Richards, 1977).

Clients may be more likely to carry out self-management programs given the presence of certain conditions:

1. The use of the self-management program will provide enough advantages or positive consequences to be worth the cost to the client in terms of time and effort. The self-management program must do more than simply meet the status quo.
2. The client's use of the program may be strengthened by enlisting the support and assistance of other persons—as long as their roles are positive, not punishing. Former clients, peers, or friends can aid the client in achieving the goals through reinforcement of the client's regular use of the self-management strategies.
3. The counselor maintains some minimal contact with the client during the time the self-management program is being carried out. Counselor reinforcement is quite important in successful implementation of self-management efforts.

You can provide reinforcement (anything that serves to increase the frequency of a desired response) easily through oral approval ("That's great," "I like that") or by knowledge of progress ("You did very well," "You did the task perfectly," "You've done a great job in improving your study habits"). Have the client drop in or telephone during the course of the self-management program. This enables you to provide immediate encouragement to the client.

WORKING WITH CLIENT INTERACTIONAL PATTERNS AND RELATIONSHIPS

With any individual client who seeks counseling, the client is part of a larger community or network, sometimes referred to as a *system*. In any interpersonal system such as a marriage, a family, a work department, or a peer group, all segments of the system are interrelated and change in the part that affects the entire system. In these systems to which the client belongs, the client typically interacts in predictable patterns. These patterns can be seen within the context of the counseling system as well as within the various systems to which the client belongs. In other words, the counselor can see the client's typical interpersonal pattern not only in the kinds of interactions the client reports with other persons but also in the way this interpersonal pattern is reenacted within the counseling relationship. Thus, in working with interactional patterns of the client, the counselor can intervene at two different levels: use of interventions that deal directly with the counselor-client system and use of interventions that impact the client's interactional style with other persons. We will describe both levels of these strategies in this portion of the chapter.

Reenactment of Interactional Patterns in Counseling

Clients begin to develop predictable interactional patterns in their family of origin. Interactional patterns are affected by many factors, including family construction and birth order (Adler, 1958), family rules and communication patterns (Watzlawick, Beavin, & Jackson, 1967), and general level of health or dysfunction of the family system (Miller, 1981; Haley, 1980). For many persons who become clients, their family of origin experience was problematic in three major ways (Teyber, 1992):

1. There was a lack of a strong bond between the parents, sometimes referred to as a lack of a "primary parental coalition" (Minuchin, 1974).
2. There were disruptions or interruptions in the ways parents met children's developmental needs for nurturance, structure, separateness, and attachment.
3. There were child-rearing practices that were either too authoritarian or too permissive in nature.

To cope with this, children, as they grow older, develop a characteristic way of interacting with others. Persons who use an Adlerian counseling model refer to this as a "lifestyle" (Adler, 1958); those who use a transactional analysis model refer to this as a "script" (Woolams & Brown, 1979). We will talk about three characteristic interpersonal patterns from a developmental/dynamic model (see also Horney, 1970). Clients generally cope in interpersonal systems by (1) moving toward people, (2) moving away or withdrawing from people, or (3) moving against or resisting other people.

People who *move toward* others are likely to be perceived by others as understanding and accommodating. These sort of people are usually helpful and cooperative but have trouble being appropriately assertive, direct, and, above all, angry. This sort of lifestyle or interpersonal pattern is designed to elicit from others the support and nurturing that was missed as a child. With a client who behaves like this toward the counselor, the counselor must be careful not just to provide acceptance but also to focus on the general interpersonal style of the client—what the client has missed from his or her family and is trying to elicit from the counselor as well as no doubt from numerous other people.

Clients who characteristically *move away or withdraw* from people will demonstrate the same behavior in the counseling relationship. They may seek help but they will attempt to maintain as much emotional distance as possible and to remain emotionally unconnected from the counseling per se. Although at one level these clients are trying to push the counselor away, at another level they want desperately for the counselor to stay connected to them. These clients pose quite a challenge for counselors. To respond reflexively and give up on the client is nontherapeutic. At the same time, if the counselor attempts to become too emotionally connected, these clients will feel alarmed and anxious. The counselor will need to stay present and engaged at a pace that follows the client's lead, but above all, the counselor must not give up on these individuals.

Clients who *move against* people are likely to try to directly intimidate the counselor or to passively resist the counselor's efforts. They may behave in ways either to take control of the session or to "push the counselor's buttons" and make the counselor feel inadequate. These kinds of clients may be especially difficult for beginning counselors who may respond countertherapeutically with fear, competition, or counterhostility (Teyber, 1992, p. 179). Again, as with the other instances we have described, it is important for the counselor not to respond reflexively and give these clients what they are trying to elicit. With these individuals, the counselor avoids getting involved in a battle or power struggle and focuses on what the clients may be trying to get and/or avoid with their interpersonal styles and the likely impact of such on their lives.

Why do clients act out their typical interactional pattern with counselors? Quite simply, it is a form of a test. They feel that the counselor will respond in the same old way as most everyone else, but they hope against hope that the counselor will provide a different and more helpful response. When the counselor does, they will not have to keep reenacting their same old pattern and can move beyond the point at which they become "stuck"— not only with the counselor but with other persons as well. Teyber presented the following brief illustration of this process.

Suppose a compliant, dependent housewife says to her male therapist, "Where should we start today?" On one hand, the therapist will fail the

*test and confirm the client's [preexisting] relational patterns if he says,
"Tell me about _____." On the other hand, the therapist will pass the test
and demonstrate that he is capable of engaging in a more egalitarian way
than the client has been able to do with her husband and father when the
therapist says, "I'd like to hear about what is most important to you. Let's
begin with something that you would like to tell me about." (1992, 181–
182)*

Teyber also noted, "Parallel to the concept of providing a 'corrective
emotional experience,' the therapist can fail this test by responding in a way
that reenacts old relational patterns, or the therapist can pass the test by
behaviorally demonstrating that relationships can be different" (1992, p.
181).

Pattern Interventions

Another level at which the counselor can respond to in the interpersonal
realm involves a change or modification in the patterns of interactions
around the interpersonal problems the client reports. This is referred to as
pattern intervention and comes from work on family therapy and
Ericksonian hypnosis (Imber-Black, Roberts, & Whiting, 1988; O'Hanlon,
1987). In the previous section, we talked about a type of pattern intervention in which the counselor attempts to change the client's characteristic
pattern by having the *counselor* respond in a new and more helpful way. In
the pattern intervention, the *client* changes something about the way he or
she interacts in a given situation with another person or group of persons.

In pattern intervention, the counselor looks for repetitive actions on the
client's part in relationships with others that are observable enough to be
modified in some way—something to the client's interpersonal pattern may
be added, deleted, or in some way varied. Typically, modifications are
made around three aspects of an interpersonal pattern: the behaviors, the
situation or context, and the sequence of behaviors (Hudson & O'Hanlon,
1991). For example, suppose you are working with a teenaged girl whose
presenting problem is that she has no friends. Upon exploring what patterns she uses in initiating and maintaining friendships, you describe that
she has made a number of new friends in the past few years but that after
several months, each friend has successively withdrawn from her, and all
have told her the same thing—that she "bugs" them. When asking her what
she thinks they mean by this, she rather openly states that she engages in a
number of "smothering" behaviors once she makes a new friend. She follows them around at school, insists they eat lunch with her, and calls them
frequently after school. Although she is supposedly trying to keep her
friends close to her, her very actions are driving them away! In pattern

interventions, you can work with helping her to modify her behaviors so that she gives her friends "space"—she requests having lunch with them only once in a while, not daily; she plans to call them perhaps once a week rather than several times a day; and so on.

In this example, you are helping the client to modify the behaviors, the context, and the sequence of her behaviors that she engages in with her friends. Of course, it is also likely that aspects of this pattern will get reenacted with you as well, so you will ultimately need to address the issue within your helping relationship as well as within her relationships with friends. The extent to which you do this, however, depends on her goals and the number of contacts or sessions that are available for working with her.

▲ EXERCISE 10.1: INTERVENTION STRATEGIES

In this exercise, three hypothetical client cases are described. After reading over each case, describe what you believe the client's probable counseling goal would be and the related intervention strategies that could be used to help each client reach these goals. Consider goals and strategies for all of the four areas we discussed in this chapter: feelings, beliefs, behaviors, and interactional patterns. You may do this activity alone, with a partner, or in a small group discussion. You may wish to exchange your responses and ideas with other helpers or share your thoughts with your instructor.

A. Case 1

Sally is an Asian American at a large university; she is overwhelmed by the size of the university, having lived in a small town all her life. She is concerned about her shyness and feels it is preventing her from making friends. She reports being uncertain about how to reach out to people. She is also concerned about her performance on tests. Although she believes her study habits are adequate, she reports that she "blows" the tests because she gets so uptight about them. She believes her grades are a reflection of herself and her family.

Probable Counseling Goals

1. _____

   _____

2. _____

   _____

Possible Counseling Strategies

1.   _____
     _____
     _____

2.   _____
     _____
     _____

B. Case 2

Mr. and Mrs. Yule have been married for two years. Both are in their sixties, and this is their second marriage; their previous spouses died within the last 10 years. Mr. and Mrs. Yule are concerned that they rushed into this second relationship without adequate thought. They report that they argue constantly about everything. They feel they have forgotten how to talk to each other in a civil manner. Mrs. Yule states that she realizes her constant nagging upsets Mr. Yule; Mr. Yule discloses that his spending a lot of time with his male buddies irritates Mrs. Yule.

Probable Counseling Goals

1.   _____
     _____

2.   _____
     _____

Possible Counseling Strategies

1.   _____
     _____
     _____

2.   _____
     _____
     _____
     _____

C. Case 3

Arthur is a third-grader at Malcolm Elementary School. He is constantly getting into trouble for a number of things and he admits that he starts a lot of fights with the other boys. Arthur says he does not know why or how, but suddenly he is punching at them. Only after these fights does he realize his anger got out of hand. Arthur realizes his behavior is causing some of the kids to avoid him, yet he believes he would like their friendship. He is not sure how to handle his temper so that he does not lash out at his peers.

Probable Counseling Goals

1. _____
   _____

2. _____
   _____

Possible Counseling Strategies

1. _____
   _____
   _____
   _____
   _____

2. _____
   _____
   _____
   _____
   _____

SUMMARY

In working with clients, all of whom present unique concerns and circumstances, you may find great use for the strategies described in this chapter. However, there are several cautions to consider in trying to use a counseling strategy effectively. The first caution in strategy implementation is to avoid oversimplification of the procedure. Although a procedure may seem relatively simple to implement, even with little experience, any therapeutic endeavor can be effective or ineffective depending on how it is administered. Second, you must practice using strategies. You will not be an expert when you first start using them, but your skill will grow as you practice. Also remember that strategies are rarely used in isolation. Several different strategies or combinations of procedures may be necessary to deal with the complexity and range of concerns presented by a single client. As an example, suppose a counselor treats a client's alcoholism but ignores the anxiety for which alcohol is used as a tranquilizer. The strategies used to decrease the drinking behavior may not be too effective unless the counselor and client also use strategies to deal with the client's limited coping skills, self-defeating thoughts, and environmental "payoffs" that maintain the drinking. (Todd & Kelley, 1972).

Finally, keep in mind that counseling is likely to be most effective when a number of these strategies are used in conjunction with one another and when the underlying counselor-client relationship contains a high level of respect and trust.

It is important to realize the limitations of counseling objectives and strategies and of counselors. One of the most frustrating experiences that counselors report is the experience of being thwarted in their attempts to help clients change and grow. Beginning counselors often approach the counseling process with a lot of zest, zeal, and unwavering idealism. Although a certain amount of this is useful, it can also lead to discouragement with oneself and with clients. Almost all clients will resist your attempts to help in some way. Some clients who see you at the request of someone else may be openly oppositional. Other clients may desire to change but because of biochemical imbalances may require medication for such things as depression or anxiety management. Clients with addictions may also find the process of recovery especially difficult. Clients from very dysfunctional systems may find the weight of the system working against their own individual efforts to change. So, as you approach your growth and development and your own efforts in working with clients, it is important to remember that there are some limits to what happens in the counseling process and that almost all client resistance to change is about fear (Teyber, 1992). As clients become more able to trust themselves and you, your efforts and theirs will be rewarded.

DISCUSSION QUESTIONS

1. In this chapter, we discuss a variety of interventions to work with the *whole person* (e.g., the client's feelings, beliefs, behaviors, and interac-

tional patterns). As you have read and worked with these interventions, which ones feel most natural and comfortable for you? Which ones do you believe you would have most trouble with?

2. What places in your own body do you consistently hold in feelings? How do you become aware of these? What do you do to release them?

3. Can you identify situations for yourself in which your beliefs have affected the way you feel and act?

4. What persons have you used in your life for role models? What are their characteristics that appeal to you?

5. How do you apply self-management to everyday behaviors for yourself?

6. What is your characteristic interactional pattern? Can you trace it back to your family of origin? How do you think this pattern will affect the way you interact with your clients?

RECOMMENDED READINGS

Bernard, M. E., & Joyce, M. R. (1984). *Rational-emotive therapy with children and adolescents.* New York: Wiley.

This is a classic book on the use of cognitive change methods for young children, teenagers, parents, and teachers.

Blechman, E. A. (1985). *Solving child behavior problems at home and at school.* Champaign, IL: Research Press.

This book offers very practical behavioral strategies to deal with typical child behavior problems.

Cormier, W. H., & Cormier, L. S. (1991). *Interviewing strategies for helpers: Fundamental skills and cognitive behavioral interventions* (3rd ed.). Pacific Grove, CA: Brooks/Cole.

This book provides an in-depth look at many counseling strategies, including cognitive restructuring, problem solving, and desensitization.

Corsini, R., & Wedding, D. (Eds.). (1989). *Current psychotherapies* (4th ed.). Itasca, IL: Peacock.

A number of various strategies based on different counseling theories are described in this book.

Ellis, A. (1987). Integrative developments in rational-emotive therapy (RET). *Journal of Integrative and Eclectic Psychotherapy, 6,* 470–479.

This article represents a recent synthesis of Ellis's A-B-C-D-E model.

Goldfried, M. R. (1988). Appreciation of rational restructuring to anxiety disorders. *The Counseling Psychologist, 16,* 50–68.

This article is a good summary of the use of cognitive restructuring to treat anxiety related problems.

Hudson, P. O., & O'Hanlon, W. H. (1991). *Rewriting love stories: Brief marital therapy.* New York: Norton.

These authors address the ways in which they use pattern interventions with couples.

Kanfer, F. H., & Goldstein, A. P. (Eds.). *Helping people change* (2nd ed.). New York: Pergamon, 1980.

A number of different authors have written excellent articles in this edited book that deals with such topics as cognitive change, self-management, modeling, and roleplay.

O'Leary, K. D., & Wilson, G. T. (1987). *Behavior therapy: Applications and outcome* (2nd ed.). Englewood Cliffs, NJ: Prentice Hall.

This is a standard and basic reference for various behavioral approaches.

Smith, E. (1992). *The body in psychotherapy.* Jefferson, NC: McFarland & Co.

This is a sophisticated and comprehensive review of body-oriented approaches to psychotherapy.

Teyber, E. (1992). *Interpersonal process in psychotherapy.* Pacific Grove, CA: Brooks/Cole.

Teyber describes a variety of approaches to working with clients' affective issues and interpersonal dynamics.

Watson, D. L., & Tharp, R. G. (1981). *Self-directed behavior: Self-modification for personal adjustment.* Pacific Grove, CA: Brooks/Cole.

This book focuses on a variety of self-directed or self-management strategies, including self-monitoring, self-reward, stimulus control, and problem solving.

Wolpe, J. (1990). *The practice of behavior therapy* (4th ed.). New York: Pergamon.

This is a classic book on behavioral strategies authored by the man who is credited as the founder of behavior therapy.

▶ 11

Receiving and Using Supervision

by Janine M. Bernard

Thus far, this book has focused on the many facets of the relationship between the counselor and client and has outlined numerous ways to enhance that relationship. At this point, we shall discuss another essential relationship in the process of helping—the relationship between the supervisor and the counselor. Our discussion will not be complete because the supervision relationship has as many potential facets as the counseling relationship. Rather, this final chapter will provide a sketch of supervision parameters with the hope that it will help you to use supervision more quickly and more fully.

THE PARAMETERS OF SUPERVISION

In order to understand supervision, we need to consider what happens in supervision, who provides the supervision, and in what context supervision occurs. It makes sense to start with a definition. Clinical supervision is

 an intervention that is provided by a senior member of a profession to a junior member or members of that same profession. This relationship is

This chapter was written for this book by Janine M. Bernard, Ph.D., Professor of Counselor Education and Director of the Community and School Counseling Program at Fairfield University, Fairfield, Connecticut.

evaluative, extends over time, and has the simultaneous purposes of enhancing the professional functioning of the junior member(s), monitoring the quality of professional services offered to the clients she, he, or they see(s), and serving as a gatekeeper for those who are to enter the particular profession. (Bernard & Goodyear, 1992, p. 4)

We will now examine this definition more closely by looking at its parts:

1. *Supervision is an intervention.* Clinical supervision is different from counseling and teaching, though it is related to both. There are competencies and skills involved in supervision that allow the supervisor to help the supervisee gain competence and insight into the dynamics of counseling. Supervision does not just happen—it is planned.

2. *Supervision is provided by a more advanced practitioner and involves evaluation.* A clinical supervisor is more advanced than the supervisee, at least on some important variables. At the same time, however, it is not always necessary that the supervisor be a highly seasoned counselor. Sometimes, a counselor who is developmentally only a couple of steps ahead of the supervisee can offer excellent feedback and direction. The important thing is that the supervisor be more advanced in the skill areas in which the supervisee needs help. Supervision also has an evaluative aspect. Except in the case of peer supervision (which could be considered consultation), supervision is conducted in part to evaluate the counselor. This *summative evaluation* will occur after there has been enough supervision to expect a certain degree of competence. However, throughout the supervision experience, there is an evaluative component. When the supervisor suggests that a counselor go in a different direction with a client, that supervisor is making a judgment regarding what has transpired during counseling up to this point. This is called *formative evaluation* and is an intrinsic part of supervision. As will be seen later in this chapter, much of the difficulty within supervision centers around the evaluative role of the supervisor.

3. *Supervision extends over time.* An important aspect of supervision is establishing some clarity regarding the supervision contract. In other words, the relationship between counselor and supervisor will be different depending on how long the two will be working together and under what conditions. An assumption of supervision, however, is that the supervision relationship will last long enough to allow for some developmental progress for the supervisee. This is important because supervision includes an assumption that counseling competency shows itself in different ways, with different clients, and in different contexts over time. For example, a person cannot assume after observing one counseling session that he or she knows the competence of the counselor. The person might be able to

evaluate the *counseling* that occurred after one session, but he or she cannot evaluate the competence of the *counselor*, at least not in any holistic way.

4. *The supervisor monitors and serves as a gatekeeper.* While conducting supervision, the supervisor is always aware that the supervisee represents only one level of the supervisor's responsibility. Ethically (and sometimes legally), the supervisor also must monitor the quality of the counseling that is being delivered to the supervisee's clients. Judgments are always being made regarding the learning goals of the counselor versus the counseling needs of the client(s). These two sets of issues provide the checks and balances that are part of supervision. Beyond serving the counselor's immediate clients, the supervisor also serves as a gatekeeper for those who want to enter the counseling profession. In doing so, the supervisor accepts some responsibility for potential future clients as well as present ones.

Responsibilities of Supervisors and Supervisees

Both the supervisee and the supervisor have certain responsibilities to each other. These responsibilities include having formally scheduled contacts with one another on a regular basis, as well as access to supervision on an as-needed basis for crises or emergencies. Another responsibility involves providing each other with information about your cases, especially the management of difficult and problematic cases. You and your supervisor are ethically obligated to safeguard the communication of your clients in a confidential manner. Additionally, your supervisor is required to track your work with clients, monitor the quality of it, and provide you with regular and periodic feedback, including suggestions for improvement. Your supervisor also is ethically bound to restrict his or her relationship with you to just supervision. In other words, during the time you are being supervised, you do not have another kind of relationship with your supervisor except for supervision. If a supervisor is also your friend, counselor, or employer, this constitutes what is referred to as a *dual relationship*, which is considered unethical by the American Counseling Association Code of Ethics (1981).

The parameters of supervision go beyond the basic elements described in the definition of supervision. For example, who can be a supervisor and in what context does supervision occur? One answer to the first of these questions is that anyone who engages in supervision is a supervisor (assuming that the supervisor meets the criteria addressed in the definition of supervision). More specifically, a clinical supervisor can be a prepracticum or a practicum instructor, a doctoral student working with graduate student trainees, or a supervisor in a field setting who works with trainees as part of their graduate internship. Once a counselor has completed graduate training, the employer, supervisor, or senior counselor in an agency, school, or other work setting may be the clinical supervisor. More and more, however, a clinical supervisor is being asked to meet certain training criteria in the practice of supervision prior to assuming the role of supervisor (Borders, Bernard, Dye, Fong, Henderson, & Nance, 1991). This has occurred as the supervision training literature has become more sophisticated.

Beyond level of experience and training in supervision, it should be noted that part of becoming a supervisor involves a *decision* to supervise. In graduate training, this decision is implicit, if not explicit, in the structure of the training program. The practicum instructor has made a decision to supervise by teaching the course. Therefore, the counselor need not be concerned about whether supervision will occur. Later on, however, as counselors enter their first professional positions, supervision may or may not be forthcoming. In such a situation, it is often up to the counselor to request supervision in order to stimulate a senior professional's decision to supervise.

Another important distinction is that between clinical supervision and administrative supervision. Your employer in a mental health center, for example, is your administrative supervisor since this person has the power to hire and/or fire you, to increase your salary, to determine your job description, and so forth. However, this person is not automatically a clinical supervisor. A clinical supervisor must be working with you in some manner to improve your counseling ability. Therefore, even a peer could be a clinical supervisor, if that person has the ability to enhance your growth and if both of you have determined to enter into a supervisory relationship. (Many advanced professionals in private practice rely on a peer supervision model with their partners in order to avoid stagnation in their work.)

THE FOCUS OF SUPERVISION

What is it that your supervisor is looking for? For beginning counselors or counselors who are working with a new supervisor, this is a common and legitimate question. Obviously, good intentions are not enough to warrant the kind of feedback a counselor hopes to receive from a supervisor, because many counselors with the best of intentions have received less than accolades from their supervisors. This section will describe the four major areas that supervisors focus on when evaluating counselor performance. Understanding the differences among these categories will help you not only to know what it is your supervisor will be looking for in your counseling but also to hear your supervisor's feedback with a more discriminating ear.

The four areas will be described as *skills* to imply that all four categories represent groups of behaviors that can be learned (to differing degrees for different people) and that can be refined. The four areas or categories are (1) process skills, (2) conceptualization skills, (3) personalization skills, and (4) professional skills (Bernard, 1979; Lanning, 1986).

Process Skills

Process skills are those overt behaviors that distinguish counseling from other social interactions. They are what you *do* in your sessions. Process skills include all *observable* counselor behaviors; therefore, the other three categories must often be inferred from the counselor's process skills. Greeting the client, requesting information, reflecting what you hear, confronting what seems to be a contradiction, structuring a roleplay, supporting a client in distress—all are process skills. Process skills range from simple (restatement) to sophisticated (paradoxical intervention), depending on the abilities of the counselor.

When a supervisor is focusing on a counselor's process skills, the feedback will sound something like this:

"I thought your initial question was a good one."

"You used a lot of questions in your session. I wonder if you could increase your use of reflections."

"Would you be willing to try a roleplay with the client?"

"Your nonverbal behavior communicated a lot of caring for the client."

Conceptualization Skills

As the term implies, *conceptualization skills* are thinking skills. Much of the covert activity of the counselor falls into this category. Conceptualization skills include identifying the major concern of the client, recognizing dominant themes in a counseling session, planning for future sessions, and choosing a particular helping response (or technique) with a certain goal in mind. Using a reflection of feeling in a counseling session is a process skill; choosing which client message to reflect is a conceptualization skill. Without adequate conceptualization skills, process skills are relatively useless because the counselor's responses, even if well executed, would be random or unrelated to what was happening in the session. Purposeful counseling occurs when the counselor conceptualizes accurately.

Supervisory statements that have as their focus the conceptualization skills of the counselor are as follows:

"When you asked about her mother, what were you looking for?"

"I thought you picked up all of the major themes in the session."

"Where are you going from here with this client?"

"Did that homework assignment accomplish what you hoped it would?"

Notice that three of the four examples of supervisor feedback were in the form of questions. This will often be the case for conceptualization skills and, similarly, for personalization skills. The supervisor can only infer what the counselor had in mind based on the process skills observed. In fact, the supervisor may not know where the counselor's skill deficit lies until such questions are answered. For example, the counselor may have asked a question when a reflection would have been far more helpful. But before the supervisor can be of help to the counselor, it must be determined whether the counselor (1) did not know how to phrase a helpful reflection (process skill deficit) or (2) did not know that a reflection was called for (conceptualization skill deficit).

Personalization Skills

The term *personalization skill* was originated to suggest that the counselor uses personal attributes, for better or for worse, in the therapeutic relationship (Bernard, 1979). The existence of such a category is an acknowledgment that counseling is indeed a very personal activity, and that it is impossible to separate your personal attributes and liabilities from your work entirely. Personalization also refers to the degree to which you have adapted to the role of helper. Therefore, personalization skills would include being comfortable with the professional responsibility of being a counselor, being able to separate your reactions to an issue from those of the client, allowing your sense of humor to emerge, not being defensive with an accusing client, being able to handle a range of emotions in yourself or when presented by the client, and being able to accept constructive criticism from your supervisor.

Possible supervisory comments that would address personalization skills are as follows:

"You were able to keep your composure, even when the client became agitated. That's good."

"It seemed to me that you almost apologized when giving the client a homework assignment, as if you didn't want to waste her time. That communicated a lack of confidence on your part. Is that how you felt?"

"When your client stated his opinions about working women with small children, I thought you stepped out of your counselor role and started arguing with him. I wondered if he was baiting you and if you did take the bait."

"You're awfully quiet whenever I give you my feedback about your last counseling session. I've been wondering what that means."

Professional Skills

Professional skills have as much to do with performance outside the counseling relationship as within (Lanning, 1986). Perhaps these skills are less noticeable in initial training experiences and more evident in later experiences. They can overlap with personalization skills (for example, being late for a counseling appointment because you are intimidated by the client) but remain a discreet category in and of themselves. These skills include turning in written reports on time, safeguarding confidentiality, behaving professionally in field placement, using others' professional titles when appropriate, dressing appropriately for counseling contacts, and related behaviors.

As you will note, some of the items listed here seem far more important than others. Safeguarding confidentiality is much more critical than not wearing jeans to see clients. On the other hand, what appears frivolous to some people may be very important to a client. If you remember that clients are in an extremely vulnerable position in asking for help, you might be more receptive to the idea that the environment within which that help is offered is intrinsically related to the help itself. For example, picture a client entering a counseling center to find three or four staff members laughing raucously. Assuming that the client is feeling somewhat ambivalent about seeking counseling, many negative thoughts could be stimulated by such a scene ("They're laughing about the client who just left"). Now assume that the counselor seeing this client is one of those jovial staff members. It is very unlikely that the counseling session that follows will be unrelated to the professional context that was presented to the client when he or she arrived.

Examples of supervisor comments that address professional skills are as follows:

"This might sound picky, but I don't think you should chew gum while you are counseling this client."

"I was pleased with how you handled the referral to the Family Counseling Center. Everything was in order."

"The last report you turned in had some grammatical errors and the use of slang. I've noted them on the report and would like you to rewrite it."

"What are you going to do if Elisabeth's teacher asks you about the content of your counseling with Elisabeth?"

Discriminating among Categories

Keeping the four categories in mind, it is important to realize that all four are present all the time in your work as a counselor. For example, as you begin a session with a new client, you will need process skills to proceed adequately; you will have thought about how you want the session to progress; you will be choosing your personal responses carefully; and you will be trying to present a professional appearance. Because all four areas are operating at all times, your supervisor is making some assumptions when choosing to focus on one category rather than the other three when giving you feedback. Perhaps an example will help make this point clearer.

In a recent supervision workshop, a videotape of a counseling session was shown in which the client teared up as she discussed a sensitive topic. When that happened, the counselor became very quiet and asked just one question for clarification. After the tape was viewed, a group of professional supervisors was asked to write down comments they would want to make to the counselor. Two of the supervisors focused on the segment of tape described above, but approached it from different angles. One said, "I wanted the counselor to say something to the client, to comfort her in some way." The other remarked, "I thought the counselor was threatened by the client's show of emotion. I would want to discuss this with her."

The first supervisor approached the issue as a process skill deficit (the counselor needed to do something that she did not do), and the second supervisor approached it as a personalization skill deficit (emotion may threaten this counselor). As you can see, the assumptions that were being made about the counselor were very different for the two supervisors.

In the situation just described, neither supervisor knew the counselor. It could make a big difference how a supervisor evaluates counseling behavior by knowing the counselor's strengths and weaknesses. On the other hand, supervisors have their own biases when observing counseling sessions; some are more likely to see events in process terms, while others are more likely to see them in conceptual terms. It is important for counselors to have some idea of the choices available to supervisors so they can appreciate the assumptions that go with those choices.

▲ EXERCISE 11.1: THE FOCUS OF SUPERVISION

For your own part, you can begin to determine the focus of your counseling sessions by asking four simple questions:

Did I know what to do in the session?
Did I know what I wanted to do?
Was I comfortable at that point?
Was my performance that of a professional counselor?

You can do this with roleplays or tapes of sessions.

STYLES OF SUPERVISION

Now that you have a better idea of what supervisors look for in training and supervising counselors, we will discuss the choices supervisors make about their own behavior. As you will soon discover, if you have not already, different supervisors have different styles. Sometimes their style makes you feel confident and supported, and sometimes their style has a less positive effect on you. At least some of this has do with the role they choose as they work with you (Bernard, 1979). By describing the different supervisory roles and their purposes, perhaps we can help you to further understand the supervision process and its potential outcomes. Perhaps we can also encourage dialogue between you and your supervisor if the role being used in your supervision is giving you problems.

The Role of Teacher

The most common role for supervisors during the initial training of counselors is the *teacher role*. (For purposes of clarification we shall use the word *instructor* to mean the person responsible for teaching a particular course, leaving the word *teacher* to mean a particular role or style the instructor may or may not wish to assume.) When in the teacher role, the supervisor takes responsibility for knowing what the counselor needs to do or learn. Therefore, the supervisor might instruct the counselor about a new technique, might model a new intervention, or might make other direct suggestions regarding the counselor's work. When the supervisor acknowledges the rightness or wrongness of a particular counselor strategy, the teacher role is being used. When a supervisor is in the teacher role, there is no question who is in charge.

Of the supervisor responses listed in the last section, several were in the teacher role. "Your nonverbal behavior communicated a lot of caring for the client," is an example of a supervisor in this role. The supervisor is taking full responsibility for knowing what is appropriate or inappropriate nonverbal behavior. Most instructional comments and evaluative comments are teacher comments.

The Role of Counselor

When supervisors focus on the interpersonal or intrapersonal dynamics of their counselors or trainees, they are most likely in the *counselor role*. The goal of the supervisor in this role is most often the personal growth of the counselor. Historically, this role has been widely used by supervisors, based on the assumption that the most legitimate way for counselors to grow professionally is to grow personally. Although the last two decades have offered differing opinions of this premise, there are times when the counselor role is the necessary and most desirable option for the supervisor to use. (It is important, however, for the supervisor to be careful to avoid a dual relationship and to suggest a referral to someone else if extensive counseling for personal issues is needed.)

Referring again to the supervisor statements listed earlier, the following is an example of a supervisor in the counselor role: "You're awfully quiet whenever I give you my feedback about your last counseling session. I've been wondering what that means." Another combined both teacher and counselor roles. See if you can identify the two roles in this comment: "It seemed to me that you almost apologized when giving your client a homework assignment, as if you didn't want to waste her time. That communicated a lack of confidence on your part. Is that how you felt?"

The Role of Consultant

When the goal of the supervisor is to encourage trainees to think on their own and to trust their own insights, the *consultant role* is most appropriate. When in this role, supervisors limit themselves to being a resource for their trainees. The authority for what will transpire in the trainee's counseling is more equally shared. As a result, the consultant role conveys a degree of mutual trust and professional respect not necessarily found in the other two roles. On the other hand, respect is the expectation that the counselor can and will put forth the effort to use this role suitably.

A consultant comment from the preceding section is: "Did that homework assignment accomplish what you hoped it would?" This is a consultant response because the supervisor is not telling the counselor that the assignment did or did not succeed. However, if the counselor answers, "Yes," and the supervisor responds, "Well, I don't agree," then the supervisor has very quickly changed from a consultant role to a teacher role.

The Need for Different Roles

One well-documented model of supervision is the *developmental model*, which describes counselor growth as advancing through sequential skill levels (Borders, 1986; McNeil, Stoltenberg, & Pierce, 1985; Stoltenberg & Delworth, 1987; Worthington, 1987). Depending on the developmental level of the counselor, different supervisor roles may be warranted.

Research indicates that trainees prefer their supervisors to be in the teacher role initially (Rabinowitz, Heppner, & Roehlke, 1986; Worthington & Roehlke, 1979). This is because they are unsure of themselves, and the teacher role gives the structure and sense of security that they need at first. After they have received considerable training, they are more likely to prefer a consultant approach. When the supervisor is in this role, it allows the counselors to stretch their wings before they assume full responsibility for their clientele. Throughout training and beyond, the counselor role may be needed (if not welcome) because trainees occasionally hit personal snags that block their therapeutic efforts.

Supervisors' roles can be deliberate or the result of personal preference or habit. Some supervisors are natural teachers and have a difficult time altering their style, even when the situation calls for it. Other supervisors keep their identity as counselors foremost in their work and approach their trainees as they would approach their clients. Finally, some supervisors like to give all trainees the opportunity to go at their own pace and prefer the consultant role. Frequently, the use of role involves a trial-and-error process. If the consultant role does not work with one trainee, then the teacher role is tried, whether or not the supervisor is aware of this change.

In the example given at the end of the previous section, the supervisor switched from consultant to teacher when the consultant role did not produce the desired response. (The supervisor obviously wanted the trainee to say that the homework did not accomplish what had been hoped.) This was not a good use of the consultant role because the supervisor was not willing to go along with the trainee's judgment. A direct teacher statement, "I don't think the homework assignment worked as you had hoped," would have been better in the long run.

You might be asking, "What if I don't like my supervisor's style? What can I do about it?" First of all, you might see if you encourage a certain role behavior. For example, if you approach supervision by asking a lot of questions, you are inviting your supervisor to assume the teacher role. If you try to convince your supervisor that you felt very anxious in your last session, you are (perhaps inadvertently) requesting the counselor role. When you make definitive statements about your work, you are encouraging a consultant role from your supervisor.

If you believe that the problem is not in your approach but due to your supervisor's preference, you can ask if another role might be tried for a while. Again, knowing about the supervision process allows you to influence it. You might want to have your supervisor in the consultant role rather than the teacher or counselor role. One counselor approached her supervisor with this request. Her supervisor's reaction was, "I think that's a good idea. I agree that I've been too active in supervision. On the other hand, if it's going to work, I think you need to come to supervision more prepared. Perhaps you could review your tapes [audiotapes of counseling sessions] ahead of time and be prepared to identify segments that gave you difficulty and give your opinion of what went wrong." The counselor found this a reasonable plan. You might have noticed that the supervisor was *teaching* the counselor how to use him as a *consultant*. This kind of transition is often needed when a change of supervision role is to occur.

As a final note, we would like to mention that many, if not most, supervisors use all three styles in their work. It is not necessary that you be able to track your supervisor's style at all times. Rather, the issue of supervision role becomes relevant when you are trying to pinpoint why you are feeling stressed under supervision or why you do not think you are progressing as quickly as you would like. The supervisor's role may or may not be the problem, but it is one more important piece of the puzzle for you to consider.

METHODS OF SUPERVISION

Now that we have discussed the different focal points in supervision and the different roles a supervisor can assume, we will comment on the methods available to supervisors to accomplish their work. Obviously, supervisors must have some way to gain access to the trainee's counseling if they are to influence it.

Self-Report

Until the introduction of technology into most counselor training programs, the most frequent form of supervision was for the counselor to report to the supervisor, either in writing or verbally, what was transpiring in counseling, and for the supervisor to react to this information as presented. This method of supervision is called *self-report* because the counselor is in control of what he or she chooses to report about the counseling session or relationship. Self-reporting is still used in supervision, though not as frequently as it once was and not as often in the initial stages of counselor training (prepracticum and practicum). When self-reporting is used, the focus is generally on conceptualization and personalization skills. A major disadvantage of self-reporting, and the reason for its decline in popularity, is that it does not allow the supervisor to help the counselor work on blind spots. Those supervisors who tend to prefer self-reporting are those who adhere theoretically to the assumption that the most salient aspect of supervision is the relationship between the supervisor and supervisee.

Audiotape, Videotape, and Live Observation

The use of audiotape, videotape, and live observation are combined here because they all involve a similar supervision approach—that of observing a trainee's counseling, followed by a critique of what was heard and seen. Most training programs prefer this form of supervision, at least in the beginning, and have some facility or laboratory for this purpose. The advantage of direct (live observation) or indirect (audio or videotape) observation is that it allows the supervisor to address the process skills that were apparent in the observed session. In addition, this method of supervision allows supervisors to compare their perceptions of what transpired in counseling with those of their counselors when the case is subsequently discussed.

Although technology can be a great aid to the supervision process, its advantages are akin to its disadvantages (Rubinstein & Hammond, 1982). For example, videotape is literally as clear as a picture, but this level of stark feedback can be either revealing or devastating to the supervisee. Audiotape is also a tremendous asset to learning, but when tapes are reviewed in a pro forma manner in the supervision session, the exercise can be fruitless. Therefore, there are two rules of thumb that are good for supervisors and supervisees to consider in using technology in supervision:

1. The vulnerability of the supervisee must be considered a part of the formula when audiotape, videotape, or live observation are used for the purposes of supervision. This does not mean that the supervisor should walk on eggshells, but it does mean that a certain level of trust and goodwill must be communicated to counter this vulnerability.
2. Case conferences using technology must be carefully planned with taped segments carefully preselected either by the counselor or by the supervisor (Bernard & Goodyear, 1992). Otherwise, an enormous amount of time can be wasted looking for the "right spot" and supervision loses its continuity and purpose.

Live Supervision

Live supervision is different from live observation in that the former includes the active participation of the supervisor during counseling.

Because live supervision is in some ways a team approach to counseling, it is typically reserved for advanced trainees. When using live supervision, the supervisor observes the session behind a one-way mirror and interrupts the session to give the counselor a suggestion. There are several ways to structure this type of supervision: (1) supervisors can phone in their suggestions using a closed-circuit phone intercommunication system; (2) supervisors can call the counselor out of the counseling room to discuss the progress of the session; (3) there can be a prearranged time (for example, 20 minutes into the session) when the counselor will leave to discuss the session with the supervisor; or (4) counselors can wear a small hearing device in their ear (referred to as a "bug in the ear") so the supervisor can make comments without interrupting the session (Bubenzer, Mahrle, & West, 1987).

Although this method of supervision has been accused of interfering with the counselor-client relationship, it offers some distinct advantages. Because the supervisor is working closely with the counselor, difficult cases can be assigned to the trainee more quickly because, in effect, the trainee is not "alone" in the counseling room. In addition, the supervisor can redirect a session that is going poorly, rather than wait until later to give the counselor remedial feedback. As a result, there is more opportunity for success from the trainee's standpoint. To date, those supervisors and counselors using live supervision have found it to be a very satisfactory method of training and of accomplishing the goals of supervision.

Simulation

Not all supervision involves actual clients. Especially in the earlier phases of training, trainees may be asked to roleplay different counseling situations in order to gain some experience prior to taking on the responsibility of seeing actual clients. When simulating, trainees are asked either to share a real concern for the purpose of training or are given a role to play with which they may or may not have had any life experience. Simulation can be used in conjunction with any of the methods of supervision described earlier.

Individual versus Group Supervision

Supervision can occur individually (one supervisor with one counselor) or in a group of counselors. Typically, the trainee will receive some of both forms during his or her training program. In individual supervision, the focus will be on the trainee exclusively, with the supervisor offering his or her expertise in ways that will benefit the individual trainee. Individual supervision is person centered. In a group, trainees usually take turns presenting one of their cases, and the group then discusses it. There is potentially more opportunity for different instructional techniques with group supervision, including roleplays (with feedback from the observers) for the purpose of practicing different approaches. Group supervision also allows the advantages of permitting trainees to learn from the cases of their peers as well as their own cases. Therefore, while individual supervision is more focused and more efficient for a particular trainee, group supervision holds the possibility of vicarious learning and a more efficient use of the supervisor's time.

AVOIDING SUPERVISION

Counseling is a very personal activity, and feedback about your counseling can be taken very personally, leaving you feeling highly anxious and threatened by the prospect of receiving supervision. It can be difficult to separate your value as a person from your success as a helper when your motivation to help is strong. Therefore, we will address the issue of avoiding supervision. Most counselors who avoid supervision do so psychologically, not physically, though there are counselors who avoid by missing or coming late to their supervision sessions.

Bauman (1972), in what now is considered a classic article, pointed out that counselors can play games to avoid dealing with their skill issues. He outlined some of the postures presented by supervisees that, in effect, help them to avoid supervision. Bauman's list of five "games" is as relevant today as it was when it was published, and includes such strategies as submission, turning the tables, "I'm no good," helplessness, and projection.

Submission

In the *submission* game, trainees yield immediately to the superior knowledge of the supervisor. Discussion is not warranted because the trainee begs out as a result of obvious inferior judgment. He or she accepts all feedback unquestioningly—almost, it seems, before hearing it. Under such conditions, the trainee communicates complete malleability and unaccountability.

Turning the Tables

We alluded to the game of *turning the tables* earlier when we discussed the counselor who solicits the teacher role from the supervisor through extensive questioning. The trainee approaches supervision as an inexhaustible source of answers to an infinite list of questions about what the supervisor suggests could have been done in the previous session. The trainee arrives at supervision well armed—but well armed to keep the supervisor at arm's length rather than well armed to learn.

"I'm No Good"

The game of *"I'm no good"* is more active than the submission strategy. Here, the trainee must convince the supervisor that he or she is on the verge of becoming a counselor casualty. The trainee magnifies counseling mistakes, placing the supervisor in the role of diminishing those self-deprecating remarks and assuring the trainee that there is hope. One possible consequence of this game is to invite the supervisor into a counselor role.

Helplessness

Yet another variation on the same theme, *helplessness* is a stance protesting lack of experience as a reason for the supervisor to take full responsibility for the direction of the trainee's counseling. In this litigious time in this profession, an increasingly common example of helplessness occurs when the trainee raises the issue of the supervisor's legal responsibility for mistakes made in the counseling session. Helpless trainees can be remarkably resourceful in their arguments.

Projection

Finally, a frequently used avoidance posture is to project the mistakes one has made in counseling onto the supervision process itself. The most salient example of *projection* is when the trainee protests that sessions that are observed by the supervisor are far more stilted and self-conscious than sessions that occur in the absence of the supervisor (or when the tape recorder is turned off). The focus of the supervision session becomes the imposition of supervision rather than the trainee's skills. And the message is that, for whatever reason, the supervisor never really sees the trainee's highly developed (or even adequate) counseling skills.

Liddle (1986) has asserted that trainee resistance stems from an attempt to avoid a perceived threat. She lists five possible sources of threat in supervision: (1) evaluation anxiety; (2) performance anxiety (living up to one's own standards of performance); (3) personal issues within the supervisee (such as having unresolved feelings about death when counseling a client who is mourning the loss of a loved one); (4) deficits in the supervisory relationship; and (5) anticipated consequences (resisting the learning of how to confront out of fear of client anger).

Does knowing about resistance help to avoid it? How do you overcome those things that threaten you in supervision? First of all, it is essential that you realize and accept that some anxiety in supervision is unavoidable (Yager, Witham, Williams, & Scheufler, 1981). We could even say that feeling no anxiety is in itself a form of avoidance. Second, you must try to identify the sources of your anxiety if you are to resolve them. If you feel yourself avoiding supervision, you might discuss this with your supervisor. Or if that's too threatening, you could find a peer you trust to help you uncover the motives or fears underlying your resistance. Finally, trainees need to find productive ways to handle their resistance rather than succumbing to a psychological avoidance of supervision. For example, pairing some of the ideas presented above, let's say that you are playing helpless with your supervisor out of a fear that learning to confront will cause client anger. Continuing to be helpless is inappropriate. However, it is highly appropriate to acknowledge your fear to your supervisor. Once you and your supervisor are dealing with the real issue, alternative strategies can be suggested. Acknowledging that you cannot counsel forever without needing the skill to confront a client, the supervisor can roleplay an angry client with you, allowing you to face your fears in a safer environment. Or if it is too threatening even to do this with your supervisor, you can perform the roleplay with one of your peers, thus gaining some experience in a nonevaluative environment. Just as there are innumerable ways for the creative but anxious trainee to avoid supervision, there are innumerable ways to help trainees conquer their fears, once those fears are accepted as a normal and legitimate part of supervision (Liddle, 1986).

A final caution: You can become as hard on yourself in your demand to be "open" in supervision as you are about your counseling skills. It is okay to hold back a little. Try not to take yourself too seriously. And remember that your supervisor was once in your position.

PREPARING FOR SUPERVISION

Yager and associates (1981) identified tips for maximizing the counselor's time in supervision. Several of their suggestions have been presented in other sections of this chapter. In addition, they offer several guidelines, such as trusting your supervisor as a most critical variable, clarifying for yourself what is most needed from supervision, communicating openly with your supervisor concerning those identified needs, and clarifying with your supervisor the content and format of supervision sessions.

Basic to all of the suggestions listed here is taking responsibility for your own supervision. There is, of course, a paradox in this suggestion, which is why it can be difficult to carry out. By the time trainees come to supervision, they have had a great deal of experience as learners. Usually this experience has taught them that they are to figure out their instructor's game plan as soon as possible and not deviate from that plan. They believe that it is their instructor's responsibility to determine what is to be learned, and that it is desirable for them to think critically within those parameters, but not to step outside the limits set by the instructor.

And yet the need to identify your own learning needs and to be able to evaluate realistically your own performance is critical to successful supervision. A trainee's inability or unwillingness to do this will hamper the supervision process. As a result, supervision represents a transition from classroom learning to professional practice. Therein lies the paradox. The most effective counseling student is the student who stops behaving like a student.

A key way that trainees show their preparedness for supervision is to evaluate themselves before each supervision session. This is equivalent to taking home the test and scoring it yourself before your instructor scores it. Even if the supervisor does not demand it (and many do), trainees should review their audiotapes (or their notes, or their recollections) to determine where supervision is most needed. Supervisors find it frustrating if they feel that they are spending more time reviewing their trainees' sessions than the trainees are. Trainees who come to supervision having prepared a rough draft of their performance evaluation are bound to gain more from the experience.

On a more mundane level, but perhaps almost as important, preparing for supervision involves being organized in all aspects of your counseling. If you plan to present an audiotape to your supervisor, be sure that the tape and the recorder work *prior to* the counseling session. If the first 10 minutes of the tape are from a former session or do not pertain to what you hope to cover, forward the tape to the appropriate spot, or write a note to go with the tape if the supervisor is to listen to it at a later time. Mark which side of the tape contains the session. Hours and hours have been wasted by frustrated supervisors when such small courtesies have been overlooked. Furthermore, taking control of these small but not insignificant details will give you a sense of control over the entire experience. This will most likely generalize to other aspects of your training experience.

▲ EXERCISE 11.2: PREPARING FOR SUPERVISION

In a small group, make a list of ways you can prepare for supervision. In a similar fashion, make a list of ways that you can increase the likelihood of using the supervision you receive in subsequent counseling sessions.

USING SUPERVISION

Just as you should come to supervision prepared to use your time productively, you should leave with a sense of direction. Going back to one of the definitions of supervision, Kutzik emphasized that the supervisor is to provide "direction that the supervisee is bound to follow" (1977, p. 5). It is entirely possible that the supervisor thinks that the implications of supervision are totally clear, but the counselor has no idea how to transfer the information gained in supervision to subsequent counseling sessions. It is even possible that the counselor is not aware that the two (counseling and supervision) should be purposefully connected.

All things being equal, translating supervision to direction for the counselor is a shared responsibility between the supervisor and the trainee. If, however, it is not clear to you how one relates to the other, you should ask before you are expected to perform again. This will avoid a common complaint made by supervisors that certain trainees are enjoyable to work with, but they do not seem to follow through on supervisory suggestions.

Even if it is clear how you are to use a supervisory suggestion, it is wise to prepare yourself sometime after supervision but before your next counseling contact. What seems perfectly clear in a discussion with your supervisor may become muddled or somehow out of reach during the counseling session if you have not integrated the concepts into your own frame of reference prior to the session. This failure to integrate is a common mistake made by trainees—one that causes them unnecessary feelings of discouragement and embarrassment. The key to maximizing supervision is to invest additional energy between supervision and subsequent counseling sessions. This will help you to avoid having to expend energy after the session to recover from disappointment of lack of success.

SUMMARY

We have addressed several of the components of supervision. Only when these operate in unison, however, does one have what is referred to as supervision. Regardless of focus, role, or method, supervision is most often described as the most rewarding part of a counselor's training. Likewise, supervisors report a high degree of satisfaction in their work with supervisees. Both parties are reflecting the distinct pleasure of passing on and safeguarding the profession of counseling.

DISCUSSION QUESTIONS

1. Everyone approaches a new experience with certain expectations. List three things you hoped to receive from supervision. List three things you know that you do not want from supervision. Discuss.

2. Looking over Bauman's list of five "games," which one do you think you are most likely to play? When you are playing this game, what should your supervisor do?

3. Most trainees receiving live supervision for the first time are nervous about how clients will react to this method. With a partner, roleplay an explanation of live supervision to a client. Give each other feedback.

4. If you were a supervisor, what trainee behavior(s) would most irritate you? What would you do about it?

RECOMMENDED READINGS

Bauman, W. F. (1972). Games counselor trainees play: Dealing with trainee resistance. *Counselor Education and Supervision, 11,* 251–256.

Bauman describes trainee resistance as five "games" and offers supervision interventions for dealing with each form of resistance.

Hawthorne, L. (1975). Games supervisors play. *Social Work, 20,* 179–183.

Hawthorne turns the tables and considers how supervisors play games. She believes that the reason for supervisor games is the supervisor's difficulty handling authority. She divides supervisor games into games of abdication and games of power.

Kadushin, A. (1968). Games people play in supervision. *Social Work, 13,* 23–32.

Similar to Bauman's article, Kadushin sees games as emerging when the student is afraid to change or fears being inadequate. Kadushin categorizes games as: (1) manipulating demand levels, (2) redefining the relationship, (3) reducing power disparity, and (4) controlling the situation. Kadushin also gives some attention to supervisor's "countergames."

Nelson, G. L. (1978). Psychotherapy supervision from the trainee's point of view: A survey of preferences. *Professional Psychology, 9,* 539–550.

Nelson reports on a study of several supervisory variables. The most noteworthy results were that trainees preferred live observation and videotaping as the method of supervision and preferred a supervisor who was flexible and interested in having the trainee develop an individualized therapeutic style.

Yager, G. G., & Beck, T. D. (1985). Beginning practicum: It only hurt until I laughed! *Counselor Education and Supervision, 25,* 149–157.

Yager and Beck enumerate several types of counselor responses that originate out of concern for competence or fear of intimacy with the client. Inappropriate counselor responses are represented in an exaggerated fashion that allows novice counselors to learn through humor.

Counseling Strategies Checklist

Most counselor trainees view the opportunity for supervision as a mixed blessing. They know that their performance has weaknesses that are more easily identified by an observer. On the other hand, they feel vulnerable at the prospect of having someone view and assess their interview behavior, particularly when they cannot see that person. There are no easy solutions to this problem. Learning to feel comfortable with your supervisor is uniquely a function of your own goals and the supervisor's awareness of your discomfort. Therefore, you must identify the implications of your counseling goals in terms of your own risk taking, and you must be prepared to communicate your fears to your supervisor.

The Counseling Strategies Checklist (CSC) is suggested as one means of assessing your performance. It is divided into categories that conform to the skills chapters in this text. The supervisor may want to use parts of the checklist for each interview, rather than attempt to complete the total checklist each time you are observed. The checklist provides a point of departure for you and your supervisor to discuss the progress of the interview, and your input and its effect on your client.

One further point might be made in reference to the use of the supervisor evaluation. It was mentioned in the text that the counselor often encounters *blocks* while attempting to respond to clients. The counselor may be able to identify quite accurately the feeling the client is describing but may not be able to respond to that feeling. This would probably be described by the Freudians as countertransference. When the client talks about a problem that is also a problem for the counselor, the counselor may feel unqualified to respond or may be overwhelmed by personal feelings and unable to respond. It is at this point that a supervisor can be most helpful in counseling the counselor, helping him or her to work through personal feelings and identifying ways to manage these feelings the next time the situation arises. To receive this assistance from your supervisor, you must acknowledge your own blockage.

HOW TO USE THE COUNSELING STRATEGIES CHECKLIST (CSC)

Each item in the CSC is scored by circling the most appropriate response, either "Yes," "No," or "N.A." (not applicable). The items are worded so that desirable responses are "Yes" or "N.A." "No" is an undesirable response.

After the supervisor has observed and rated the interview, the two of you should sit down and review the ratings. Where noticeable deficiencies exist, you and the supervisor should identify a goal or goals that will remedy the problem. Beyond this, you should list two or three action steps that permit you to achieve the goal. After three or four more interviews, have the supervisor evaluate you again, and compare, the two sets of ratings to determine whether or not progress was evident.

Part I: Counselor Reinforcing Behavior (Nonverbal)

1. The counselor maintained eye contact with the client.

   Yes   No   N.A.

2. The counselor displayed several different facial expressions during the interview.

   Yes   No   N.A.

3. The counselor's facial expressions reflected the mood of the client.

   Yes   No   N.A.

4. The counselor often responded to the client with facial animation and alertness.

   Yes   No   N.A.

5. The counselor displayed intermittent head movements (up-down, side-to-side).

   Yes   No   N.A.

6. The counselor refrained from head nodding when the client did not pursue goal-directed topics.

   Yes   No   N.A.

7. The counselor demonstrated a relaxed body position.

   Yes   No   N.A.

8. The counselor leaned forward as a means of encouraging the client to engage in some goal-directed behavior.

   Yes   No   N.A.

9. The counselor demonstrated some variation in voice pitch when talking.

   Yes   No   N.A.

10. The counselor's voice was easily heard by the client.

    Yes   No   N.A.

11. The counselor used intermittent one-word vocalizations ("mm-hmm") to reinforce the client's demonstration of goal-directed topics or behaviors.

    Yes   No   N.A.

Counselor Reinforcing Behavior (Verbal)

12. The counselor usually spoke slowly enough so that each word was easily understood.

    Yes   No   N.A.

13. A majority (60 percent or more) of the counselor's responses could be categorized as complete sentences rather than monosyllabic phrases.

    Yes   No   N.A.

14. The counselor's verbal statements were concise and to the point.

    Yes   No   N.A.

15. The counselor refrained from repetition in verbal statements.

    Yes   No   N.A.

16. The counselor made verbal comments that pursued the topic introduced by the client.

    Yes   No   N.A.

17. The subject of the counselor's verbal statements usually referred to the client, either by name or the second-person pronoun, *you*.

Yes   No   N.A.

18. A clear and sensible progression of topics was evident in the counselor's verbal behavior; the counselor avoided rambling.

Yes   No   N.A.

Part II: Opening the Interview

1. In the first part of the interview, the counselor used several different nonverbal gestures (smiling, head nodding, hand movement, etc.) to help put the client at ease.

Yes   No   N.A.

2. In starting the interview, the counselor remained silent or invited the client to talk about whatever he or she wanted, thus leaving the selection of initial topic up to the client.

Yes   No   N.A.

3. After the first five minutes of the interview, the counselor refrained from encouraging social conversation.

Yes   No   N.A.

4. After the first topic of discussion was exhausted, the counselor remained silent until the client identified a new topic.

Yes   No   N.A.

5. The counselor provided structure (information about nature, purposes of counseling, time limits, etc.) when the client indicated uncertainty about the interview.

Yes   No   N.A.

6. In beginning the *initial* interview, the counselor used at least one of the following structuring procedures:
   a. Provided information about taping and/or observation
   b. Commented on confidentiality
   c. Made remarks about the counselor's role and purpose of the interview
   d. Discussed with the client his or her expectations about counseling

Yes   No   N.A.

Part III: Termination of the Interview

1. The counselor informed the client before terminating that the interview was almost over.

   Yes   No   N.A.

2. The counselor refrained from introducing new material (a different topic) at the termination phase of the interview.

   Yes   No   N.A.

3. The counselor discouraged the client from pursuing new topics within the last five minutes of the interview by avoiding asking for further information about it.

   Yes   No   N.A.

4. Only one attempt to terminate the interview was required before the termination was actually completed.

   Yes   No   N.A.

5. The counselor initiated the termination of the interview through use of some closing strategy such as acknowledgment of time limits and/or summarization (by self or client).

   Yes   No   N.A.

6. At the end of the interview, the counselor offered the client an opportunity to return for another interview.

   Yes   No   N.A.

Part IV: Goal Setting

1. The counselor asked the client to identify some of the conditions surrounding the occurrence of the client's problem (*"When* do you feel _____?").

   Yes   No   N.A.

2. The counselor asked the client to identify some of the consequences resulting from the client's behavior ("What happens when you _____?").

   Yes   No   N.A.

3. The counselor asked the client to state how he or she would like to change his or her behavior ("How would you like for things to be different?").

   Yes   No   N.A.

4. The counselor and client decided *together* on counseling goals.

   Yes   No   N.A.

5. The goals set in the interview were specific and observable.

   Yes   No   N.A.

6. The counselor asked the client to orally state a commitment to work for goal achievement.

   Yes   No   N.A.

7. If the client appeared resistant or unconcerned about achieving change, the counselor discussed this with the client.

   Yes   No   N.A.

8. The counselor asked the client to specify at least one action step he or she might take toward his or her goal.

   Yes   No   N.A.

9. The counselor suggested alternatives available to the client.

   Yes   No   N.A.

10. The counselor helped the client to develop action steps for goal attainment.

    Yes   No   N.A.

11. Action steps designated by counselor and client were specific and realistic in scope.

    Yes   No   N.A.

12. The counselor provided an opportunity within the interview for the client to practice or rehearse the action step.

    Yes   No   N.A.

13. The counselor provided feedback to the client concerning the execution of the action step.

    Yes   No   N.A.

14. The counselor encouraged the client to observe and evaluate the progress and outcomes of action steps taken outside the interview.

    Yes   No   N.A.

Part V: Counselor Discrimination

1. The counselor's responses were usually directed toward the most important component of *each* of the client's communications.

   Yes   No   N.A.

2. The counselor followed client topic changes by responding to the primary cognitive or affective idea reflecting a common theme in each communication.

   Yes   No   N.A.

3. The counselor usually identified and responded to the feelings of the client.

   Yes   No   N.A.

4. The counselor usually identified and responded to the behaviors of the client.

   Yes   No   N.A.

5. The counselor verbally acknowledged several (at least two) nonverbal affect cues.

   Yes   No   N.A.

6. The counselor encouraged the client to talk about his or her feelings.

   Yes   No   N.A.

7. The counselor encouraged the client to identify and evaluate his or her actions.

   Yes   No   N.A.

8. The counselor discouraged the client from making and accepting excuses (rationalization) for his or her behavior.

   Yes   No   N.A.

9. The counselor asked questions that the client could not answer in a yes or no fashion (typically beginning with words such as *how, what, when, where, who,* etc.).

   Yes   No   N.A.

10. Several times (at least two) the counselor confronted the client with a discrepancy present in the client's communication and/or behavior.

    Yes   No   N.A.

11. Several times (at least two) the counselor used responses that supported or reinforced something the client said or did.

    Yes   No   N.A.

12. The counselor used several (at least two) responses that suggested a course of action the client had the potential for completing in the future.

    Yes   No   N.A.

13. Sometimes the counselor restated or clarified the client's previous communication.

    Yes   No   N.A.

14. The counselor used several (at least two) responses that summarized ambivalent and conflicting feelings of the client.

    Yes   No   N.A.

15. The counselor encouraged discussion of negative feelings (anger, fear) expressed by the client.

    Yes   No   N.A.

16. Several times (at least two) the counselor suggested how the client might feel about a particular topic.

    Yes   No   N.A.

Part VI: The Process of Relating

1. The counselor made statements that reflected the client's feelings.

   Yes   No   N.A.

2. The counselor responded to the core of a long and ambivalent client statement.

   Yes   No   N.A.

3. The counselor verbally stated his or her desire and/or intent to understand.

   Yes   No   N.A.

4. The counselor made verbal statements that the client reaffirmed without qualifying or changing the counselor's previous response.

   Yes   No   N.A.

5. The counselor made attempts to verbally communicate his or her understanding of the client that elicited an affirmative client response ("Yes, that's exactly right," and so forth).

    Yes   No   N.A.

6. The counselor reflected the client's feelings at the same or a greater level of intensity than originally expressed by the client.

    Yes   No   N.A.

7. In communicating understanding of the client's feelings, the counselor verbalized the anticipation present in the client's communication (i.e., what the client would like to do or how the client would like to be).

    Yes   No   N.A.

8. The counselor frowned when failing to understand what the client was saying.

    Yes   No   N.A.

9. The counselor verbalized personal confusion or misunderstanding to the client.

    Yes   No   N.A.

10. The counselor nodded when agreeing with or encouraging the client.

    Yes   No   N.A.

11. When the counselor's nonverbal behavior suggested that he or she was uncertain or disagreeing, the counselor verbally acknowledged this to the client.

    Yes   No   N.A.

12. The counselor answered directly when the client asked about his or her opinion or reaction.

    Yes   No   N.A.

13. The counselor encouraged discussion of statements made by the client that challenged the counselor's knowledge and beliefs.

    Yes   No   N.A.

14. Several times (at least twice) the counselor shared his or her own feelings with the client.

    Yes   No   N.A.

15. At least one time during the interview the counselor provided specific feedback to the client.

    Yes   No   N.A.

16. The counselor encouraged the client to identify and discuss his or her feelings concerning the counselor and the interview.

    Yes   No   N.A.

17. The counselor voluntarily shared his or her feelings about the client and the counseling relationship.

    Yes   No   N.A.

18. The counselor expressed reactions about the client's strengths and/or potential.

    Yes   No   N.A.

19. The counselor made responses that reflected his or her liking and appreciation of the client.

    Yes   No   N.A.

References

Adler, A. (1958). *What life should mean to you.* New York: Capricorn.

American Counseling Association. (1981). *Ethical standards* (rev. ed.). Alexandria, VA: Author.

American Association for Marriage and Family Therapy. (1985). *Code of ethical principles for marriage and family therapists.* Washington, DC: Author.

American Psychological Association. (1992). *Ethical principles of psychologists* (rev. ed.). Washington, DC: Author.

Bandura, A. (1969). *Principles of behavior modification.* New York: Holt, Rinehart and Winston.

Banikiotes, P. G., Kubinski, J. A., & Pursell, S. A. (1981). Sex role orientation, self-disclosure, and gender-related perceptions. *Journal of Counseling Psychology, 28,* 140–146.

Barrett-Lennard, G. T. (1981). The empathy cycle: Refinement of a nuclear concept. *Journal of Counseling Psychology, 28,* 91–100.

Bauman, W. F. (1972). Games counselor trainees play: Dealing with trainee resistance. *Counselor Education and Supervision, 11,* 251–256.

Beck, A. T. (1976). *Cognitive therapy and the emotional disorders.* New York: International Universities Press.

Bellack, A., Rozensky, R., & Schwartz, J. (1974). A comparison of two forms of self-monitoring in a behavioral weight reduction program. *Behavior Therapy, 5,* 523–530.

Benjamin, A. (1987). *The helping interview* (4th ed.). Boston: Houghton Mifflin.

Bernard, J. M. (1979). Supervisor training: A discrimination model. *Counselor Education and Supervision, 19,* 60–68.

Bernard, J. M., & Goodyear, R. K. (1992). *Fundamentals of clinical supervision.* Boston: Allyn and Bacon.

Borders, L. D. (1986). Facilitating supervisee-growth: Implications of developmental models of counseling supervision. *Michigan Journal of Counseling and Development, 17,* 7–12.

Borders, L. D., Bernard, J. M., Dye, H. A., Fong, M. L., Henderson, P., & Nance, D. W. (1991). Curriculum guide for training counseling supervisors: Rationale, development, and implementation. *Counselor Education and Supervision, 31*, 58–80.

Bornstein, P. H., & Devine, P. A. (1980). Covert modeling and hypnosis in the treatment of obesity. *Psychotherapy: Theory, Research and Practice, 17*, 272–275.

Brammer, L. M., Shostrom, E. L., & Abrego, P. J. (1989). *Therapeutic psychology: Fundamentals of counseling and psychotherapy* (5th ed.). Englewood Cliffs, NJ: Prentice Hall.

Branden, N. (1971). *The disowned self.* Los Angeles: Nash Publishing.

Bubenzer, D. L., Mahrle, C., & West, J. D. (1987). *Live counselor supervision: trainee acculturation and supervision interventions.* Paper presented at the Annual Convention of the American Association for Counseling and Development, New Orleans, LA.

Cautela, J. R. (1969). Behavior therapy and self-control: Technique and implications. In C. Franks (Ed.), *Behavior therapy: Appraisal and status* (pp. 323–340). New York: McGraw-Hill.

Ciminero, A., Nelson, R., & Lipinski, D. (1977). Self-monitoring procedures. In A. Ciminero, K. Calhoun, & H. Adams (Eds.). *Handbook of behavioral assessment* (pp. 195–232). New York: Wiley.

Corey, G. (1991). *Theory and practice of counseling and psychotherapy* (4th ed.). Pacific Grove, CA: Brooks/Cole.

Corey, G., Corey, M. S., & Callanan, P. (1988). *Issues and ethics in the helping professions* (3rd ed.). Pacific Grove, CA: Brooks/Cole.

Cormier, L. S., & Hackney, H. (1987). *The professional counselor.* Englewood Cliffs, NJ: Prentice Hall.

Cormier, L. S., & Hackney, H. L. (1992). *The professional counselor: A process guide to helping.* Boston: Allyn and Bacon.

Cormier, W. H., & Cormier, L. S. (1991). *Interviewing strategies for helpers: Fundamental skills and cognitive behavioral interventions* (2nd ed.). Pacific Grove, CA: Brooks/Cole.

Decker, R. J. (1988). *Effective psychotherapy: The silent dialogue.* New York: Hemisphere.

Egan, G. (1976). *Interpersonal living: A skills/contract approach to human relations training in groups.* Monterey, CA: Brooks/Cole.

Egan, G. (1990). *The skilled helper* (4th ed.). Pacific Grove, CA: Brooks/Cole.

Ekman, P., & Friesen, W. V. (1967). Head and body cues in the judgment of emotion: A reformulation. *Perceptual and Motor Skills, 24*, 711–724.

Ekman, P., & Friesen, W. V. (1969). Non-verbal leakage and clues to deception. *Psychiatry, 32*, 88–105.

Forrest, D. V. (1983). Employee assistance programs in the 1980s: Expanding career options for counselors. *Personnel and Guidance Journal, 62*, 105–107.

Fretz, B., Corn, R., Tuemmler, J., & Bellet, W. (1979). Counselor nonverbal behaviors and client evaluations. *Journal of Counseling Psychology, 26*, 304–311.

Friedlander, M. L., & Phillips, S. D. (1984). Stochastic process analysis of interactive discourse in early counseling interviews. *Journal of Counseling Psychology, 31,* 139–148.

Garfield, S. L. (1986). An eclectic psychotherapy. In J. C. Norcross (Ed.), *Handbook of eclectic psychotherapy.* New York: Brunner/Mazel.

Ginott, H. (1965). *Between parent and child.* New York: Avon.

Greenberg, L. S., & Goldman, R. I. (1988). Training in experiential therapy. *Journal of Consulting and Clinical Psychology, 56,* 696–702.

Greenberg, L. S., & Safran, J. P. (1981). Encoding and cognitive therapy: Changing what clients attend to. *Psychotherapy: Theory, Research and Practice, 18,* 163–169.

Haley, J. (1980). *Leaving home.* New York: McGraw-Hill.

Hansen, J. C., Stevic, R. R., & Warner, R. W. (1982). *Counseling: Theory and process* (4th ed.). Boston: Allyn and Bacon.

Harper, R., Wiens, A., & Matarazzo, J. (1978). *Nonverbal communication: The state of the art.* New York: Wiley.

Hill, C. E., Siegelman, L., Gronsky, B., Sturniolo, F., & Fretz, B. (1981). Nonverbal communication and counseling outcome. *Journal of Counseling Psychology, 24,* 92–97.

Horney, K. (1970). *Neurosis and human growth.* New York: Norton.

Hosford, R., & deVisser, L. (1974). *Behavioral approaches to counseling: An introduction.* Washington, DC: American Personnel and Guidance Association.

Hosford, R., Moss, C., & Morrell, G. (1976). The self-as-a-model technique: Helping prison inmates change. In J. D. Krumboltz and C. E. Thoresen (Eds.), *Counseling methods* (pp. 487–495). New York: Holt, Rinehart and Winston.

Hudson, P. O., & O'Hanlon, W. H. (1991). *Rewriting love stories: Brief marital therapy.* New York: Norton.

Hutchins, D., & Cole, C. (1992). *Helping relationships and strategies* (2nd ed.). Pacific Grove, CA: Brooks/Cole.

Imber-Black, E., Roberts, J., & Whiting, R. (Eds.). (1988). *Rituals in families and family therapy.* New York: Norton.

Ivey, A. E., Ivey, M. B., & Simek-Downing, L. (1987). *Counseling and psychotherapy: Integrating skills, theory, and practice* (2nd ed.). Englewood Cliffs, NJ: Prentice Hall.

Ivey, A. E., with Simek-Downing, L. (1980). *Counseling and psychotherapy: Skills, theories, and practice.* Englewood Cliffs, NJ: Prentice Hall.

Johnson, D. W. (1986). *Reaching out* (3rd ed.). Englewood Cliffs, NJ: Prentice Hall.

Jourard, S. M. (1963). *Personal adjustment.* New York: Macmillan.

Kanfer, F. H. (1980). Self-management methods. In F. H. Kanfer & A. P. Goldstein (Eds.), *Helping people change* (2nd ed.) (pp. 334–389). New York: Pergamon.

Karasu, T. B. (1992). *Wisdom in the practice of psychotherapy.* New York: Basic Books.

Karen, R. (1992). Shame. *Atlantic Monthly, 269,* 40–70.

Karoly, P., & Kanfer, F. A. (Eds.). (1982). *Self-management and behavior change.* New York: Pergamon.

Kazdin, A. E. (1976). Effects of covert modeling, multiple models, and model reinforcement on assertive behavior. *Behavior Therapy, 1,* 211–222.

Kazdin, A. E. (1982). The separate and combined effects of covert and overt rehearsal in developing assertive behavior. *Behavior Therapy and Research, 20,* 17–25.

Kelley, C. (1974). *Education in feeling and purpose.* Vancouver, WA: The Radix Institute, c/o C. Kelley, 13715 Southeast 36th St., Vancouver, WA 98684.

Kelley, C. R. (1979). Freeing blocked anger. *The Radix Journal, 1* (3), 19–33.

Knapp, M. L., (1978). *Nonverbal communication in human interaction* (2nd ed.). New York: Holt, Rinehart and Winston.

Kottler, J. (1991). *The compleat therapist.* San Francisco: Jossey-Bass.

Kutzik, A. J. (1977). The medical field. In F. W. Kaslow (Ed.) *Supervision, consultation, and staff training in the helping professions.* San Francisco: Jossey-Bass.

Lanning, W. (1986). Development of the supervisor emphasis rating form. *Counselor Education and Supervision, 25,* 191–196.

Lazarus, A. (1966). Behavioral rehearsal vs. non-directive therapy vs. advice in effecting behavior change. *Behavior Research and Therapy, 4,* 209–212.

Lazarus, A. (1976). *Multimodal behavior therapy.* New York: Springer.

Lewis, H. B. (1971). *Shame and guilt in neurosis.* Lido Beach, NY: International Universities Press.

Liddle, B. J. (1986). Resistance in supervision: A response to perceived threat. *Counselor Education and Supervision, 26,* 117–127.

Lietaer, G. (1984). Unconditional positive regard: A controversial basic attitude in client-centered therapy. In R. F. Levant & J. M. Schlien (Eds.), *Client-centered therapy and the person-centered approach: New directions in theory, research and practice.* New York: Praeger.

Lowen, A. (1965). *Breathing, movement, and feeling.* New York: Institute for Bioenergetic Analysis.

McFall, R. (1977). Parameters of self-monitoring. In R. Stuart (Ed.), *Behavioral self-management: Strategies, techniques, and outcomes* (pp. 196–214). New York: Brunner/Mazel.

McKeachie, W. J. (1976). Psychology in America's bicentennial year. *American Psychologist, 31,* 819–833.

McMullin, R. E. (1986). *Handbook of cognitive therapy techniques.* New York: Norton.

McNeil, B. W., Stoltenberg, C. D., & Pierce, R. A. (1985). Supervisees' perceptions of their development: A test of the counselor complexity model. *Journal of Counseling Psychology, 32,* 630–633.

Mahl, G. F. (1963). The lexical and linguistic levels in the expression of emotions. In M. H. Knapp (Ed.), *Expressions of the emotions in man.* New York: International University Press.

Mahoney, M., Moura, N., & Wade, T. (1973). The relative efficacy of self-reward, self-punishment, and self-monitoring techniques for weight loss. *Journal of Consulting and Clinical Psychology, 40,* 404–407.

Mehrabian, A. (1968). Communications without words. *Psychology Today, 2,* 53–55.

Meichenbaum, D. (1974). *Therapist manual for cognitive behavior modification.* Unpublished manuscript, University of Waterloo, Ontario, Canada.

Mellody, P. (1989). *Facing codependence.* New York: Harper & Row.

Melnick, J. (1973). A comparison of replication techniques in the modification of minimal dating behavior. *Journal of Abnormal Psychology, 81,* 51–59.

Miller, A. (1981). *The drama of the gifted child.* New York: Basic Books.

Miller, S. (1985). *The shame experiment.* Haberford, PA: Analytic Press.

Miller, S., Wackman, D., Nunnally, E., & Miller, P. (1988). *Connecting with self and others.* Littleton, CO: Interpersonal Communication Programs.

Minuchin, S. (1974). *Families and family therapy.* Cambridge, MA: Harvard University Press.

National Association of Social Workers. (1979). *Code of ethics.* Washington, DC: Author.

Nelson, R. (1977). Methodological issues in assessment via self-monitoring. In J. D. Cone & R. P. Hawkins (Eds.), *Behavioral assessment: New directions in clinical psychology* (pp. 217–254). New York: Brunner/Mazel.

Nelson, R., Lipinski, D., & Boykin, R. (1978). The effects of self-recorders' training and the obtrusiveness of the self-recording device on the accuracy and reactivity of self-monitoring. *Behavior Therapy, 9,* 200–208.

Nilsson, P., Strassberg, D., & Bannon, J. (1979). Perceptions of counselor self-disclosure: An analogue study. *Journal of Counseling Psychology, 26,* 399–404.

O'Hanlon, W. H. (1987). *Taproots:. Underlying principles of Milton H. Erickson's therapy and hypnosis.* New York: Norton.

Ohlsen, M. M. (Ed.). (1983). *Introduction to counseling* (pp. 133–144). Itasca, IL: Peacock.

Patterson, C. H. (1985). *The therapeutic relationship: Foundations for an eclectic psychotherapy.* Monterey, CA: Brooks/Cole.

Perls, F. (1969). *Ego, hunger, and aggression.* New York: Vintage.

Perls, F. S. (1973). *The gestalt approach and eyewitness to therapy.* Palo Alto, CA: Science and Behavior Books.

Perri, M. G., & Richards, C. S. (1977). An investigation of naturally occurring episodes of self-controlled behaviors. *Journal of Counseling Psychology, 24,* 178–183.

Premack, D. (1965). Reinforcement theory. In D. Levin (Ed.), *Nebraska symposium on motivation* (pp. 123–180). Lincoln: University of Nebraska Press.

Rabinowitz, F. E., Heppner, P. O., & Roehlke, H. J. (1986). Descriptive study of process and outcome variables of supervision over time. *Journal of Counseling Psychology, 33,* 292–300.

Rogers, C. (1957). The necessary and sufficient conditions of therapeutic personality change. *Journal of Counseling Psychology, 21,* 95–103.

Rogers, C., & Truax, C. B. (1967). The therapeutic conditions antecedent to change: A theoretical view. In C. R. Rogers (Ed.), *The therapeutic relationship and its impact.* Madison: University of Wisconsin Press.

Rubinstein, M., & Hammond, D. (1982). The use of videotape in psychotherapy supervision. In M. Blumenfield (Ed.), *Applied supervision in psychotherapy* (pp. 143–164). New York: Grune & Stratton.

Simpkinson, A., & Simpkinson, C. (1992). Man talk/woman talk. *Common Boundary,* Jan./Feb., 30–33.

Smith, E. (1985). *The body in psychotherapy.* Jefferson, NC: McFarland.

Steinem, G. (1992). *Revolution from within: A book of self-esteem.* Boston: Little, Brown.

Stoltenberg, C. D., & Delworth, U. (1987). *Supervising counselors and therapists: A developmental approach.* San Francisco: Jossey-Bass.

Sue, D. W. (1992). The challenge of multiculturalism: The road less traveled. *American Counselor, 1,* 6–15.

Sue, D. W., & Sue, D. (1977). Barriers to effective cross-cultural counseling. *Journal of Counseling Psychology, 24,* 420–429.

Tannen, D. (1990). *You just don't understand.* New York: Random House.

Taussig, I. M. (1987). Comparative responses of Mexican-Americans and Anglo-Americans to early goal-setting in public mental health clinics. *Journal of Counseling Psychology, 34,* 214–217.

Teyber, E. (1992). *Interpersonal process in psychotherapy* (2nd ed.). Pacific Grove, CA: Brooks/Cole.

Todd, F. J., & Kelley, R. J. (1972). *Behavior complexity, behavior analysis and behavior therapy.* Unpublished paper, University of Colorado Medical Center.

Tyson, J. A., & Wall, S. M. (1983). Effect of inconsistency between counselor verbal and nonverbal behavior on perceptions of counselor attributes. *Journal of Counseling Psychology, 30,* 433–437.

Utz, P. W. (1983). Counseling college students. In M. Ohlsen (Ed.), *Introduction to counseling.* Itasca, IL: Peacock.

Walen, S. R., DiGuiseppe, R., & Wessler, R. L. (1980). *A Practitioner's guide to rational-emotive therapy.* New York: Oxford University Press.

Watson, D., & Tharp, R. (1972). *Self-directed behavior change: Self-modification for personal adjustment,* Monterey, CA: Brooks/Cole.

Watson, D., & Tharp, R. (1981). *Self-directed behavior change: Self-modification for personal adjustment.* Monterey, CA: Brooks/Cole.

Watson, O. M. (1970). *Proxemic behavior: A cross-cultural study.* The Hague: Mouton.

Watzlawick, P., Beavin, J. H., & Jackson, D. D. (1967). *Pragmatics of human communication.* New York: Norton.

Wilson, G. T. (1989). Behavior therapy. In R. Corsini & P. Wedding (Eds.), *Current psychotherapies* (4th ed.) (pp. 241–289). Itasca, IL: Peacock.

Woolams, S., & Brown, M. (1979). *TA: The total handbook of transactional analysis.* Englewood Cliffs, NJ: Prentice Hall.

Worthington, E. L., Jr. (1987). Changes in supervision as counselors and supervisors gain experience: A review. *Professional Psychology: Research and Practice, 18,* 189–208.

Worthington, E. L., Jr. & Roehlke, H. J. (1979). Effective supervision as perceived by beginning counselors-in-training. *Journal of Counseling Psychology, 26,* 64–73.

Yager, G. G., Witham, M. V., Williams, G. T., & Scheufler, C. E. (1981). *Tips for the inexperienced counselor: How to maximize your time in supervision.* Paper presented at the North Central Association for Counselor Education and Supervision Annual Meeting, Milwaukee, WI.

Index